FUZZY MATH

THE ESSENTIAL GUIDE TO THE BUSH TAX PLAN

ALSO BY PAUL KRUGMAN

The Age of Diminished Expectations

Peddling Prosperity

Pop Internationalism

The Accidental Theorist

The Return of Depression Economics

FUZZY

THE ESSENTIAL GUIDE TO THE BUSH TAX PLAN

MATH

PAUL KRUGMAN

W. W. NORTON & COMPANY

NEW YORK LONDON

For information about permission to reproduce selections from this book, write to
Permissions, W. W. Norton & Company, Inc., 500 Fifth Avenue, New York, NY 10110

The text of this book is composed in Bembo
with the display set in Bauer Bodoni Titling and Meta Normal
Composition by Gina Webster
Manufacturing by The Courier Companies, Inc.
Book design by Chris Welch
Production manager: Andrew Marasia

ISBN 0-393-05062-9

W. W. Norton & Company, Inc., 500 Fifth Avenue, New York, N.Y. 10110
www.wwnorton.com

W. W. Norton & Company Ltd., Castle House, 75/76 Wells Street, London W1T 3QT

1 2 3 4 5 6 7 8 9 0

CONTENTS

PART III: MAKING THE CUT

INTRODUCTION

THIS BOOK IS NOT a mystery novel, so let me start by giving away the ending. Is the tax cut being proposed by George W. Bush a good idea? No. It is much too large, even given optimistic forecasts of future surpluses. And it is all the more irresponsible given the high probability that those forecasts, like all long-run budget forecasts in the past, will turn out to be wrong.

Will the tax cut destroy America's prosperity? Probably not. As Adam Smith observed, there's a deal of ruin in a nation. We have a huge, resilient economy that can survive and recover from even quite bad government policies.

Yet while the tax cut may not be a matter of economic life or death, it is a very serious issue. For one thing, like it or not, the tax cut has become the central political issue in the United

States right now. Conservatives who want to reshape America view passage of a large tax cut as a first step toward realizing their vision. For that reason, those who do not share this vision feel, rightly, that they must oppose the plan.

The drive for tax cuts also has a dire influence on the rest of policymaking, distorting the debate on many other subjects. How should we respond to the current economic slowdown? We can't discuss that rationally, because the administration insists that the slowdown this year justifies a huge tax cut over the next ten years, and it won't allow proposals for a temporary tax cut to boost the economy to be considered separately from its long-run proposals. How should we deal with the need to extend Medicare to include prescription drugs? The administration cannot present a realistic plan, because that would too obviously cut into the large surplus it claims is available for tax cuts. How should we plan our defense policy? The administration cannot discuss this objectively, because the numbers that would emerge would cast doubt on the affordability of the tax cut . . . well, you get the point.

And it's not just a matter of concrete proposals. There's something about the tax cut crusade that gives the crusaders a disdain for petty concerns, like telling the truth about their own proposals. Maybe they feel that the end justifies the means, or maybe they feel that white lies don't matter in the service of a higher truth. Whatever the reason, the arguments made for tax cuts have been startling in their intellectual dishonesty. One might dismiss the untrue things Bush said during the campaign as par for the political course—though I don't know of any campaign in modern times that has been quite so cynical in its misrepresentations. But what has happened since Bush moved to Washington—the deliberate misstatements and suppression of the facts—is, as far as I know, unprecedented in the history of American economic policy. It would be a shame if this style of governing succeeds, because it will set a precedent for future administrations.

The debate over tax cuts also provides an opportunity for a kind of civics lesson, one that is badly needed. It has become clear that even people who should know better—for example, reporters and television commentators—don't understand the basics about the federal government: where the money comes from, where it goes, how Social Security works. And if the voters are also confused, one can hardly blame them: most people are focused not on politics but on their daily lives, our politicians have done their best to confuse us, and our press has done nothing to keep the politicians honest. But perhaps the tax cut debate offers an opportunity to get beyond catchphrases like "big government" and "protecting Social Security" and to have a genuine debate about what we want and what we don't want the government to do, and how society should pay for the things we want. On a more personal note, this book offers me an opportunity for a longer form of discussion that can't be squeezed into 735-word columns in the *New York Times*.

Since this book is in part a civics lesson, it begins with the deep background: the political logic that has made tax cuts such an imperative for conservatives even though they are not a popular cause, and the economic impact—real and imagined—of tax cuts in general. It then moves on to shallower background: the realities of the U.S. budget as it is, the origins and plausibility (or lack thereof) of those huge surplus forecasts for the next decade, and the long-run perspective. Only then do I move on to the tax cut proposals on the table: the Bush plan and the alternatives.

Obviously this book has a point of view. But it is not a diatribe: it is intended to be a "citizen's guide." As we will see, there is a case for tax cuts; there is even a case for the Bush tax cut, though it is not the case the administration is making. The main purpose of this book is to inform; what you do with that information is up to you.

PART I

IS LESS MORE?

1

THE POLITICS OF
TAX CUTS

T HE ENGLISH-SPEAKING world has a long tradition of
tax revolt. From Wat Tyler's rebellion against Richard
II's poll tax in the fourteenth century to the truckers'
protest against high gasoline taxes that paralyzed Britain for
several days last year, there have been many occasions on
which ordinary people have risen up against what they see as
excessive taxation.

This is not one of those occasions.

The politics of today's tax cut debate in the United States
are peculiar. The people aren't much interested in the subject.
Those who *are* interested in the subject often have views that
are contrary to their personal financial interests. But in an
important sense this is not really a debate about money. It is
rather about how history will be written, about whether the

son can escape from the shadow of the father, about "creating facts" today that will determine what kind of society we are a generation from now.

I have no particular expertise in political analysis. But we can't discuss the economics of tax cuts without some sense of the political context; so let me offer a brief, personal overview of how I think about the politics of tax cuts.

An Indifferent Public

Although the tax cut proposal was the centerpiece of George W. Bush's campaign, and passing that tax cut intact has become Bush's main priority since taking power, polls have consistently suggested that voters at large have never been very interested in receiving that tax cut. Other issues, notably protecting Social Security, have a much firmer grip on the public's attention. It is true that recently, with full use of the bully pulpit, Bush has managed to get a poll or two suggesting that people think that a tax cut is important, but this reflects less people's desire for a personal tax cut than his success in convincing some of them that a tax cut would promote economic recovery. And a large majority still think that his tax cut proposal is too big, and too tilted toward the rich.

You might dismiss the opinion polls and say that in the poll that counted, the actual election, the people did choose the candidate who promised the big tax cut. But there are a few problems with that argument—and not just the obvious one, that more people voted for Al Gore. Studies of the election suggest that the traditional voting pattern, in which higher-income people vote for tax cutters and lower-income people vote for big spenders, broke down in 2000. Many people in the lower half of the income distribution—people who would, as we'll see, get little or no tax break under the Bush plan—voted Republican; many people in the top few percent of the distribution, who would be the big beneficiaries of the Bush tax cut, voted Democratic.

The most spectacular divergence between personal economic interest and political views has emerged since the election, with a group of billionaires led by Warren Buffet speaking out against one feature of the tax plan, elimination of the estate tax, that is almost entirely a benefit for the wealthy. It was a mark of the strangeness of this debate that an editorial in *Investor's Business Daily* attacked these billionaires as selfish—after all, many of them won't pay much estate tax. The editorial neglected to point out that the reason they won't pay much tax is that they intend to leave most of their estates to charity.

My opinion is that those who voted for Bush did so mainly for cultural reasons—that they saw him as a defender of traditional values against a godless modern world, that they perceived themselves as voting for a regular guy against the representative of a condescending elite. Those chants of "no fuzzy math" that greeted Gore's hapless attempts to convince voters that Bush's plan was tilted toward the rich were surely fueled less by desire for tax cuts than by resentment against people who, in the eyes of the chanters, thought that they were smarter than ordinary folks.

But Bush could have tapped into that resentment in other ways. Why take the risk of basing his campaign on a tax cut that, as we'll see, really is tilted strongly toward the rich and is more or less impossible to shoehorn into a responsible budget proposal?

Sins of the Father

For conservatives, no pedestal is high enough for Ronald Reagan. I've recently encountered several references to Reagan as one of our "three greatest presidents," which leaves me wondering whom we're supposed to demote: George Washington, Abraham Lincoln, or Franklin Roosevelt?

Of course, this is entirely understandable. The right in the United States hadn't really had a president it could call its own since 1932. Republicans had often occupied the White House, but they had not tried to roll back the expansion of government under the New Deal and the Great Society. Richard Nixon, in particular, was a raving liberal by current political standards, someone under whom federal spending on civilian programs expanded rapidly, under whom environmental and safety regulation became notably more stringent.

Reagan was the first president who tried to reverse the growth of government. And the three landslide electoral victories of 1980, 1984, and 1988 seemed to conservatives to confirm that their movement had history on its side.

Then George Bush the elder did the unforgivable: he lost.

It used to be hard for those of us not in the conservative movement to appreciate just how angry, how dismayed the right was at the loss of the next two elections—why many Republicans in Congress refused to refer to Bill Clinton as "the president," at best calling him "*your* president." After Florida, it's a bit easier to empathize. They felt that they had been denied what was rightfully theirs. The tide of history was supposed to be running in their direction—and then, through the ineptitude of their candidates and the personal charm of that awful man in the White House, they had been sent into cruel exile.

Bush the elder took much of the blame. After all, he was the apostate—the man who promised "read my lips: no new taxes," then, out of a misplaced sense of presidential responsibility, reneged on that pledge.

The campaign of Bush the younger began with his father's men—with veterans of the first Bush administration, many of them now powerful corporate chieftains, who saw the camera-ready Texas governor as the man who could avenge their defeat. But to get the Republican party as a whole behind him, Bush had to convince the Reagan loyalists, who felt that his father had let down the cause, that he was another Ronald Reagan, not another George Bush.

It's hard to believe now, but in the early days of the battle for the Republican nomination magazine heir Steve Forbes was widely regarded as a serious contender, and certainly as a threat to Bush. Forbes's signature issue was his proposal to replace the progressive income tax with a "flat tax," which puts all taxpayers, no matter how high their incomes, in the same tax bracket. And Forbes, claiming the Reagan legacy, was not shy about making parallels between father and son, accusing the younger Bush in particular of having tried to raise taxes in Texas.

What Bush had actually proposed for Texas was a plan reminiscent of Margaret Thatcher's policies in Britain. He wanted to cut corporate and property taxes—"progressive" taxes that fall more heavily on those with higher incomes—while raising the sales tax, a "regressive" tax that falls more heavily on those with lower incomes. In effect he proposed cutting taxes on the rich while raising them on the poor and the middle class. That was too raw, even for Texas, and the plan did not get enacted.

It was in response to this challenge that the Bush tax plan—not a flat tax, but a move in Forbes's general direction—was introduced early in the presidential campaign. The plan has not changed in any important way since then.

Bush's inflexibility on his tax plan, his insistence that despite all the changes in the economic situation since 1999 the plan he proposed then is "just right," is understood best in terms of this political background. Bush cannot expand his plan without raising fiscal alarms; even as it stands now he is able to make budget numbers add up only through highly creative accounting. But he cannot shrink it either without seeming to be just like his father, talking conservative on the campaign trail but going all moderate when in office.

All of this makes perfect sense given that there is a powerful wing of the Republican party that sees tax cuts as a litmus test, the issue that determines whether a politician is really part of the movement. But where does this attachment to tax cuts come from?

Fight the Future

One reason conservatives want tax cuts is, of course, that they believe that lower taxes will lead to faster economic growth. We'll look at this strictly economic argument in the next chapter. But the conservative case for tax cuts goes deeper; it rests on political economy as well as simple economics.

A defining feature of the conservative agenda is the desire for smaller government. Conservatives would like to see Lyndon Johnson's Great Society and maybe even Franklin Roosevelt's New Deal rolled back, and certainly do not want to see the United States become *more* of a welfare state, to become more like Sweden or Canada.

One way to promote smaller government is directly: you can oppose proposals for new programs and try to cut existing programs. But you can also work toward that goal indirectly, by making sure that future politicians find it hard to pay for social programs.

Ronald Reagan's budget director, David Stockman, famously— or is it infamously?—admitted, first to a journalist and later in his own book, that Reagan's advisers never really believed in the "rosy scenario" under which the 1981 tax cut would be easily affordable. Instead they sought to use the threat of deficits as a club with which to beat down spending. And though they obviously did not succeed in curbing spending enough to prevent the emergence of huge deficits, one has to admit that the persistent deficits of the next 15 years did make our government more penny-pinching, that by cutting taxes Reagan "created facts" that forced his successors to keep government smaller than it might otherwise have been. Conversely, the emergence of surpluses in the late 1990s contributed to a noticeable loosening of the reins, again not nearly enough to offset the rise in revenue, but enough to change the political dynamic.

So an important reason why conservatives want to cut taxes is that they want to keep the federal government hungry; they don't want money readily available to finance new programs, or even to maintain old ones.

And some conservatives are playing an even deeper game: they believe that they can permanently alter the nation's political economy, creating a self-reinforcing cycle of government downsizing.

Maybe the easiest way to understand this idea is to look at the contrast between politics in Canada and in the United States. Canada's government is much larger compared with the size of its economy than that of the United States: in 1997 government at all levels spent 42 percent of GDP in Canada, 32 percent in the United States. This means that in Canada taxes are considerably higher, and social programs are considerably more generous. Yet in the United States voters and politicians routinely complain about "big government," while in Canada they don't. Canadian counterparts to the American right do exist, and do win elections in some places, but are far less influential. In terms of its politics, Canada is far more like Europe than it is like the United States.

Why is the political landscape south of the border so different? One answer has to be the great American distinction: race. Let's say it bluntly: in the United States the beneficiaries of social programs tend to be a different color than the beneficiaries of tax cuts. To take an all-too-relevant example, a majority of both African American and Hispanic families with children would receive no tax cut at all under the Bush tax plan. And surely this racial divide influences the attitude of middle-income voters toward any program that seems to redistribute income downward; they are that much less likely, on seeing a poor person, to think "There but for the grace of God go I."

But conservative political theorists have a more benign interpretation of the American difference. They believe that big government and small government both tend to be self-reinforcing. Suppose, they say, that a country has a Canadian-type government, with high taxes on the affluent and expansive social programs. Then many, even most voters receive aid from the government that is worth more than they pay in taxes; so they will be inclined to think that a big government is a good thing. (In fact, some estimates have found that a majority of Canadians are net recipients of government funds.) On the other hand, start with a smaller government with a less progressive tax system, where the median voter pays noticeably more in taxes than he or she receives in benefits, and most voters will see government as a burden rather than a help, and vote to make it even smaller.

From this point of view, the Clinton years weren't just an aberration, they threatened to permanently shift the whole trajectory of American politics. Tax rates on the rich rose but rates on middle-income families did not, the economy prospered, and people started to feel better about their government. The dream of rolling back the welfare state was in danger of perishing.

The goal, then, is to put the United States firmly back on the right side of the tipping point. If you think about the conservative agenda this way, you can see immediately that it must go beyond tax cuts; ultimately it must go after our two big middle-class social programs, Social Security and Medicare, and either eliminate them or transform them into essentially private systems. Proposals to partially privatize Social Security are therefore an integral part of the larger vision, and a step on the road to bigger things.

But tax cuts are the first step, and you can see now why they are so central to conservatives and why getting his tax cut is so important to George W. Bush.

Most people, of course, neither know nor care about such grand visions. For them the important question is whether the proposed tax cuts will help them, and whether they will help the economy.

2

THE ECONOMICS
OF TAX CUTS

SERIOUS ENTHUSIASTS FOR tax cuts see high taxes as the root of all economic evil, and maybe of all evil, period. One of the ideologues behind Ronald Reagan's tax cut was a *Wall Street Journal* editorial writer turned tax cut evangelist named Jude Wanniski, whose book decrying high taxes was modestly titled *The Way the World Works*.

And if high taxes are the root of all evil, tax cuts are a magic elixir, one that will make sick economies healthy and make healthy economies prosper all the more. Tax cut proponents are nothing if not consistent. During the campaign George W. Bush was asked whether there were any circumstances under which he might reconsider his tax cut proposal—for example, what if growth were to slow, and the surpluses he proposed to return to taxpayers were to disappear? In that case, he declared, we should cut taxes anyway, to stimulate the economy.

As my survey of the politics of tax cuts might have suggested, this is not a symmetric debate. The proponents of tax cuts always think that such cuts are a terrific idea, almost regardless of the state of the economy or of anything else. The mirror-image position, as far as I can tell, doesn't exist. I can't think of anyone who is opposed to tax cuts under all circumstances, who cannot even for the sake of argument envision a situation in which cutting taxes is a good idea. In particular, it's more or less impossible to find an economist who will deny that taxes impose *some* drag on the economy, both in the short run and in the long run. And almost everyone agrees that under some circumstances tax cuts can be, if not a magic elixir for the economy, part of a sound medicinal regime. Tax cut skeptics don't disagree with the proposition that there are times and places when tax cuts are appropriate; they just don't think that this is the time or the place.

Demand-Side Economics: Tax Cuts and Recessions

Every once in a while the economy loses momentum. For whatever reason—high interest rates, a slump in stock prices, a spike in energy prices—businesses and families become reluctant to spend money. And because one man's purchase is another man's sale, the result is declining production and rising unemployment. This is what we call a recession; if it is deep enough and goes on long enough, we call it a depression.

In principle, recessions eventually cure themselves. Sometimes this automatic cure occurs quickly: businesses work off excess inventories and crank up their production again, and consumers get the urge to resume spending. If there isn't a quick turnaround, gradual processes will eventually solve the problem: as prices fall in the face of a depressed economy, the purchasing power of the cash in circulation will rise, eventually impelling the public to do something with that cash—spend it themselves, or lend it out, which will push down interest rates and persuade other people to spend. In the long run recessions are self-correcting.

But as the great economist John Maynard Keynes remarked, in the long run we are all dead. Keynes argued that when the economy slumps it is the government's job to get people spending again, to bring the economy rapidly out of a slump. And as Richard Nixon rather prematurely declared 30 years ago, we are all Keynesians now (it wasn't true when he said it, but it *is* true now). Even those who revile the name of Keynes, whom they vaguely and wrongly imagine to have been a leftist, now offer policy prescriptions that are, whether they know it or not, entirely Keynesian in spirit.

What can the government do to get people spending again? Tax cuts are one possible answer: leave more money in the hands of consumers, and they will probably spend at least some of it. Though nobody talks about it these days, government spending is another answer, indeed a more certain one: you can't be sure how much, if any, of a tax break people will choose to spend, but if the government hires workers to dig ditches and pour concrete, it knows that it will directly create those jobs and indirectly create others when the newly employed workers spend their wages. Last but not least, the government—or more accurately the Federal Reserve, which is not exactly part of the government—can try to get people to spend by reducing interest rates.

Among these alternatives, which one should you reach for first? That was the subject of a classic economic debate in the 1950s and 1960s, one that was more or less won by "monetarists" led by Milton Friedman, who argued that it was better to rely on monetary policy—cutting interest rates to fight a recession—than on fiscal policies like tax cuts or spending increases. (There was a lot more to the debate than that, but the rest need not concern us here.) Recession fighting, in other words, was the job of the Fed, not the Treasury.

But the debate has reemerged lately, with a strange political twist. Milton Friedman, while he is a great technical economist, is also a passionate political partisan. And his monetarist doctrine was as much about his conservative politics as it was about economic analysis. Friedman and his followers emphasized the primacy of monetary over fiscal policy partly because they wanted to undermine the argument that government spending is good because it creates jobs. (Modern liberals rarely make that argument, but you can still see it in the writings of people like John Kenneth Galbraith.) And this was, as I said, an argument that Friedman and his followers more or less won; as we'll see in a minute, there is a very good case for assigning the job of fighting recessions mainly to the Fed.

But then the right switched sides! Nowadays conservatives extol the virtue of tax cuts and budget deficits as ways of fighting recession; and in support of their position they offer elaborately specious arguments, worthy of a big-spending Keynesian half a century ago, about why monetary policy is ineffective.

My favorite example came when Lawrence Lindsey, Bush's chief economist, tried to demonstrate that a tax cut has more "heft" than an interest rate cut by pointing out how little impact Fed policy has on credit card bills—as if that were the main channel of monetary influence.

There's no mystery about why the right switched sides in this debate: it was sheer political opportunism. If you admit that monetary policy is a highly effective policy tool, you are very close to giving credit for the economic boom that started in late 1982 to the Fed's dramatic interest rate cuts the preceding summer, not to the tax cut pushed through by Ronald Reagan the year before. And that would detract from the Reagan legend, which plays such a crucial role in conservative mythology. More recently, members of the Bush administration have jumped on the prospect of an economic slowdown like football players piling onto a fumbled ball, claiming that it is a reason to pass their tax cut proposal immediately, no questions asked. Again, the original conservative view that monetary policy is the right tool for dealing with recessions undercuts a politically convenient argument for Bush.

But leaving political maneuvering aside, what is the economic theory of the case?

The mainstream view among economists, which was the conservative view until politics dictated otherwise, is that monetary policy and fiscal policy are like aspirin and morphine. Both are painkillers, but when you feel a headache coming on you reach for the aspirin first. It's quicker and easier to use, good enough for most purposes, and not addictive. You use morphine only under special circumstances—only when the usual, over-the-counter painkillers fail and only when you have a very good reason to run the risk of using something dangerous.

The economic argument goes like this. In the United States, as in most advanced countries, interest rates are controlled not by the government proper but by a "central bank" that is neither exactly part of the government nor exactly outside it. Our central bank, the Federal Reserve, is headed by Chairman Alan Greenspan, who is widely—and correctly—credited with preventing the stock market slump of 1987 from causing a recession, with getting the nation out of the recession of 1990–91, and with preventing the world financial crisis of 1998 from spiraling out of control.

The reason the credit goes to Greenspan, rather than to the elected politicians who were serving during each moment of crisis, is that the Fed is invariably the first line of defense against the threat of an economic slowdown. For one thing, the Fed can act quickly—when the Fed's Open Market Committee changes the interest rate that decision takes effect instantly. The Open Market Committee normally meets to consider interest rates every eight weeks, and it can move more quickly than that in emergencies. Under Greenspan the Fed has not been shy about moving rates up or down when circumstances seem to warrant such moves, because it knows that its mistakes can be reversed quickly. For example, suppose that after an interest rate cut the economy comes roaring back, faster than anyone expected: the Fed would waste no time putting interest rates back up again.

Finally, perhaps the crucial point: the Fed is uninhibited about changing interest rates because these are relatively non-political decisions. Yes, there are always voices clamoring for cheap money while others demand stern monetary discipline. But debates about whether interest rates should go up or down are much less fraught politically than debates over taxes and government spending, since there is never a question about *whose* interest rates will be cut. Furthermore, the Fed is institutionally insulated from political pressure: most Fed officials are professionals who serve long terms, not political appointees. The relative absence of politics from its discussions is the big reason why the Fed can move quickly to head off recessions.

Every reason I have just given why interest rate cuts are a good way to respond to garden-variety economic slowdowns is a reason why tax cuts are a bad way to respond. Tax cuts take time—time to debate legislation, time to put the legislation into effect. It takes many months for even the most expedited tax cut to have an impact on actual paychecks. And tax cuts are hard to reverse when conditions change: try to imagine this Congress, or any Congress, passing a tax cut this year, then deciding to take it back early next year in the face of an unexpectedly strong recovery. So like morphine, tax cuts tend to be addictive. And it's not news to say that debates over how much to cut whose taxes involve a bit of politics.

The same critique applies, but with even more force, to government spending programs. So you can now see why mainstream economists have accepted Friedman's view that monetary, not fiscal, policy should be the tool of choice for stabilizing the economy.

Is there ever a good economic case for using tax cuts to fight a business slowdown? Yes: tax cuts—and/or government spending—can be useful in those rare cases in which monetary policy unaided is not up to the job of turning the economy around. In the 1930s the United States was caught in what is known as a "liquidity trap": interest rates had been reduced almost to zero, yet that was insufficient to pull the economy out of the Great Depression; it took a massive public works program, otherwise known as World War II, to do the trick. For a long time this story seemed like ancient history, but a few years ago Japan stumbled into a 1930s-style liquidity trap. In Japan interest rates have been close to zero for years, yet the economy remains depressed; the only thing that has kept the economy from going into a full-blown depression is deficit spending by the government. So in principle it is possible for a country to find itself in a situation in which cutting interest rates, even all the way to zero, isn't enough; when you suspect that this might be the case, other policies, including tax cuts, become useful additional tools. When the pain is just too great to handle with aspirin alone, you bring out the morphine.

We're not in a Japanese-style economic trap now, but in the face of falling stock prices, nervous consumers, and a feeling among some businesses that they invested too much in recent years, such a trap has become conceivable. (Not likely, but conceivable.) Given this, there is a case—not an open-and-shut argument, but a reasonable case—to be made for offering some immediate tax cut now as a way of warding off even the possibility of getting into such a trap. As I said earlier, there *are* arguments for a tax cut; this is one of them.

Having said that, we need to ask whether the Bush tax cut proposal can be justified that way. This gets us a bit ahead of our story; we'll come back to it in more detail in Chapter 9. But let's say it now: the tax cut proposed by the Bush administration does not look anything like a recession-fighting measure. If the current slowdown were your main concern, you would want the tax cut to be "front-loaded"—that is, you should deliver big tax breaks soon, when you want people to spend more, and not commit to offering huge tax breaks years later, when the economy may have recovered and be suffering from too *much* spending. In fact, however, the Bush tax cut is heavily "back-loaded"—the initial tax breaks are very small, and the numbers don't really get big until the second half of the decade. What will the state of the economy be in 2006? Nobody has the faintest idea.

Nor can this deficiency be easily fixed by accelerating the tax cut. For one thing, the plan still commits the government to big tax breaks years in the future, which have nothing to do with the current downturn. More important, the administration has been reluctant to propose large immediate tax cuts, because that would push the already alarming long-run cost of the tax plan even higher. In a perverse but predictable way, the commitment to big tax cuts in the long run inhibits the consideration of immediate tax cuts that would be large enough to be useful right now.

But then maybe tax cutting *should* be justified only by long-run considerations, not as a tool of short-run economic management. Indeed, that is more or less the orthodox economists' line: leave short-run stabilization up to the Fed, and base your tax policy on long-run concerns. The question then becomes: Can we find a long-run justification for tax cuts?

Supply-Side Economics: Tax Cuts and Long-Run Growth

A Nobel Prize–winning expert on taxation once explained that the reason he was a professor was that it was a nice life, and that was something the government hadn't figured out how to tax. The joke illustrated one of the main principles of his field: taxes on any given activity deter that activity. Italians drive smaller cars than Americans partly because high taxes on gasoline discourage them from driving big cars; Americans drink less wine than Italians partly because high taxes on alcoholic beverages discourage them from having wine with dinner.

This is standard, uncontroversial textbook economics. And few economists would disagree with the broader statement that taxes deter economic activity, because they reduce the incentives to work hard, invest, and take risks. If we could figure out a way to pay for the government services we want without taxing ourselves, our GDP would be larger. And to the extent that we can find a way to reduce taxes without compromising other goals, we can also help the economy grow.

Notice that this case for tax cuts is not the same as the "demand-side" argument for tax cuts I described in the first part of this chapter. We're not talking now about cutting taxes as a way to get people to spend more, to put the economy's productive capacity back to work. We're talking about cutting taxes as a way to induce people to work harder, save more, and take bigger risks, thereby *expanding* that productive capacity. In other words, we're talking about enhancing the economy's supply side, not its level of demand.

Every economist believes that the supply side is important and that taxes reduce the incentives to be economically productive. But since the 1970s the term "supply-side economics" has been reserved not for this uncontroversial view but for an extreme position, one that claims that tax reductions from the levels currently prevailing in the United States would have enormous positive effects on the willingness of workers to work, investors to invest, and so on. Supply-siders believe, in particular, that in proposing tax cuts we need not be worried about the effects of those cuts on the government's budget balance. They insist that a tax cut would stimulate the economy so much that the government's tax take would actually rise, or at least that the economy would grow so much that any deterioration in the government's finances would be no cause for concern.

Since every economist believes that taxes have *some* supply-side effect, we aren't talking about issues of principle here. Rather, it's a question of numbers: how much would a cut in taxes from the levels currently prevailing in the United States actually matter to the country's long-run economic growth? This question can only be settled by looking at the evidence. Not that one can hold a serious discussion with the supply-siders themselves; just as tax cutters cannot imagine any situation in which tax cuts would be a bad idea, supply-siders never concede that any evidence actually contradicts their beliefs. Still, the rest of us can look at the record.

And the record offers little support for a strong view about the effect of tax cuts on the economy's supply side. Yes, Reagan's 1981 tax cut was followed by an economic boom. But much of the credit for that boom—a rapid recovery from the devastating recession of 1979–82—goes to the Fed, which abruptly switched from a tight-money policy to an easy-money policy in the summer of 1982. Moreover, the boom was not a supply-side event but a demand-side recovery, a surge in consumer and business spending that allowed the economy to put workers back to work and get factories running again.

If you look for evidence of anything beyond that demand-side recovery in the Reagan record, you will find it very elusive. One way to measure growth in the economy's productive capacity is to look at growth rates between "business cycle peaks," times when the economy seems to be working at full capacity. Such peaks occurred in 1973, 1979, 1990, and 2000. As Table 1 shows, the growth rate from the peak in 1979 to that in 1990 was basically the same as that between the previous two peaks. In other words, at the end of the Reagan expansion the economy's productive capacity was just about what you would have predicted if you had extrapolated from the capacity growth that took place during the Ford and Carter years. Where's the supply-side effect?

Capacity growth picked up a bit during the 1990s. And therein lies the most decisive argument against an extreme supply-side view. Bill Clinton introduced a clearly anti–supply-side policy in 1993: he engineered a substantial increase in the "top marginal rate"—the rate that high-income taxpayers pay on each extra dollar of income. This is the tax rate that supply-siders most want to reduce, because they think that it is the rate that discourages individuals from trying to become rich. Surely if they were right about the negative effects of high taxes on the rich, Clinton's action would have slowed economic growth. Instead, growth began to accelerate.

Even more telling, while the economic expansion under Ronald Reagan looked like a simple increase in demand, the expansion under Clinton did not. When an economy recovers from a demand-side slump, you expect growth to be fast at first, but then to slow down as the economy runs out of slack to take up. As we see in Table 1, that's what happened in the 1980s, but it did not happen in the 1990s. In the later Clinton years growth surged in an economy that was already prosperous, that was already more or less at full employment. In other words, it was Clinton, not Reagan, who presided over a true supply-side boom, an increase in the productive capacity of the economy.

Notice my choice of words: "presided over," not "caused." Clinton didn't cause the supply-side boom of the late 1990s; he just happened to be there when it happened. The same can be said of Reagan's role in the less-impressive demand-side boom of the mid-1980s.

The main lesson of the past 20 years about tax cuts and long-run economic growth is a negative one. Although we all believe that changes in tax rates must have *some* impact on long-run economic growth, that impact is invisible in the

Table 1

U.S. ECONOMIC GROWTH RATES, SELECTED PERIODS (IN PERCENT)		
From peak to peak	*The "Reagan expansion"*	*The "Clinton expansion"*
1973–1979: 3.0	1982–1986: 4.6	1991–1996: 3.2
1979–1990: 2.9	1986–1990: 3.2	1996–2000: 4.3
1990–2000: 3.2		

Source: Economic Report of the President.

record. Reagan's tax cut didn't cause the economy's underlying growth to accelerate in the 1980s; Clinton's tax increase didn't prevent that underlying growth from accelerating in the 1990s. The bottom line is that at the levels of taxation currently prevailing in the United States, the supply-side effects of either tax cuts or tax increases on economic growth must be modest or their effects would be more noticeable in the economic record.

Still, one could try to make a supply-side case for the Bush tax plan. The plan is, after all, basically shaped by supply-side ideology—remember that it was originally crafted to fight off a feared challenge from Steve Forbes. That supply-side ideology explains why the plan is, as we'll see, heavily tilted toward the rich: when your goal is to increase the incentive to *become* rich, it's very hard to avoid also giving big benefits to those who already *are* rich. But for some reason Bush has not made his case in terms of supply-side arguments.

So we have a remarkable scene: the administration, having committed itself to a plan that can be justified only in terms of supply-side ideology, never refers to that ideology in its efforts to sell the plan. We never hear the argument that tax cuts will produce an acceleration in the rate at which the economy's productive capacity grows. Instead the administration claims virtues for its tax plan that have nothing to do with the reasons why the plan was originally proposed, or why it has the structure it does. So it should not be surprising that those claims don't have much to do with reality.

PART II

FOLLOW THE MONEY

3

GETTING AND SPENDING

THE FEDERAL BUDGET

WAS TALKING POLITICS with a doctor—a well-educated, affluent man, the sort of person you would expect to be fairly knowledgeable about the world. And he startled me: when the talk turned to the federal budget, he declared that we could surely make room for tax cuts by cutting back on all that money the United States gives in foreign aid.

For the record: about 0.6 percent of the federal budget goes for foreign aid, and half of that consists of military assistance to our allies—that is, it really should be considered part of our defense budget. But the doctor was under the impression that humanitarian foreign aid is a big-ticket item in the federal budget, comparable in size to defense spending or Medicare. And he was also under the impression that the United States is a generous aid giver, when in fact we are the Scrooges of the advanced world, giving a smaller percentage of our national income in aid than any other major advanced nation.

Alas, his belief in that particular urban legend is not unusual. Polls suggest that most voters think that foreign aid is around 15 percent of federal spending—about 25 times larger than it actually is. But there are many other misconceptions. On the left, you find people who believe that defense still dominates federal spending the way it did when Eisenhower was president. On the right, you find people who believe that a large share of their hard-earned money goes to support welfare queens driving Cadillacs.

If we want to discuss tax cuts rationally, we have to start with a realistic picture of the federal budget. Where does the money come from? Where does it go? And how should we think about the government's role in our society?

Taking It In: The Federal Tax System

There are lots of federal taxes, but three taxes—the income tax, the payroll tax, and the corporate profits tax—account for the bulk of the revenues. Let's look at each of them in turn.

The income tax. The biggest tax, of course—though not by much—is the one that comes due every April 15. Last year the income tax collected just over $1 trillion.

In the 1980s it seemed as if the income tax might actually fall into second place, behind the payroll tax. During the Reagan administration income tax rates were greatly reduced, while payroll tax rates went up sharply. But income tax receipts rose rapidly during the 1990s, for several reasons. Bill Clinton partially reversed the Reagan tax cut, raising tax rates on high-income taxpayers in 1993; the tax take also grew along with the economy. But there were two other reasons why the income tax has been providing Washington with a lot of revenue lately: growing income inequality and a booming stock market.

Increasing income inequality is good for income tax revenues because the income tax is highly "progressive"—it is structured so that families with high incomes pay a much larger share of their income in income taxes than families with low incomes. In fact, about a quarter of families pay no income tax at all; families near the middle of the income distribution pay about 5 percent of their income in income taxes; and families in the top 1 percent of the distribution pay more than 20 percent of their income in federal income taxes. Now, for the past two decades, for reasons that are much debated, the distribution of income in the United States has become increasingly unequal. About half of all income taxes are paid by families in the top 5 percent of the income distribution; between 1990 and 1999, while the real income of the average family rose only 15 percent, the real income of the top 5 percent rose 35 percent. Since the income of the families that pay most of the income tax grew much more rapidly than that of other families, it's not surprising that income tax revenue has also grown much more rapidly than the economy as a whole.

The other big source of surging income tax receipts has

been a soaring stock market. Capital gains—the money people make by reselling stocks at prices higher than they originally paid—count as taxable income. And since almost anyone who sold a stock during the great bull market of the 1990s sold it for a much higher price than he or she originally paid, taxes on capital gains contributed mightily to federal coffers. As you may have noticed, things have changed on that front; but the fiscal results of the bear market in stocks haven't yet become visible in the tax take.

The payroll tax. If you look at the stub on your paycheck, you will notice a large deduction labeled "FICA." This is the payroll tax, the one that funds Social Security and Medicare—or rather half of it, since the other half is paid, at least nominally, by your employer.

The payroll tax is levied on all employees at a rate of 15.3 percent; while part of it, which is dedicated to Medicare, is applied to all earnings, most of it applies only to earnings up to a maximum annual income that has gradually been increased over time, and now stands at more than $76,000. Since most people earn less than that, the payroll tax on the majority of Americans is 15.3 percent. On paper half the tax is paid by the employee, half by the employer. I say "on paper" because there is almost universal agreement among tax experts that the division of the tax between the employer's share and the employee's share is a distinction with no difference: since it's up to the employer to fork over 15.3 percent of each employee's wage to the government, it makes no difference that half of that sum appears on the pay stub and the other half does not.

So who really pays the payroll tax? Is the payroll tax reflected in reduced profits for the employer or in reduced wages for the worker? Again, there is generally universal agreement that the real burden of the tax falls almost entirely on the worker. Basically, an employer will only hire a worker if the cost *to the employer* of hiring that worker is no more than the value that worker can add. So a worker is paid roughly what he or she adds to the value of production, *minus* the payroll tax; in effect, the whole tax is deducted from wages.

If we agree that the payroll tax is basically a tax on workers' wages—and to repeat, this is not a controversial view; it is the view of the vast majority of analysts—then we immediately arrive at a striking conclusion: although the income tax collects more money than the payroll tax, most American families pay considerably more in payroll taxes than they do in income taxes. The reason is that everyone pays that 15.3 percent tax on the first $76,000 of their income—which is more than most families make. On the other hand, most American families pay less than 15 percent of their income in income taxes. In 1999, a family of four with an income of $35,000 and no special deductions like mortgage payments paid only 7 percent in income taxes, less than half its payroll tax burden; even a family with an income of $70,000 paid only 13 percent of income in income taxes, still less than its payroll taxes. A recent study by the Congressional Budget Office confirmed that 80 percent of families pay more in payroll taxes than they do in income taxes.

On the other hand, for very affluent families the payroll tax is a minor issue, while income taxes are a major issue. Someone making a million dollars pays only a few percent of his income in payroll taxes, because aside from the Medicare component the tax applies only to the first $76,000 of that income. Meanwhile he is likely to pay more than 20 percent of his income in income taxes.

You can already guess where this leads us: because the Bush tax plan cuts income taxes but leaves payroll taxes unchanged, it automatically gives its biggest benefits—measured either as a share of income or as a share of total tax payments—to people who pay much more in income taxes than they do in payroll taxes: people with very high incomes.

The corporate profits tax. The corporate profits tax is the third major federal tax, taking in slightly more than $200 billion last year. Like the income tax, it has surged in recent years thanks to a boom in corporate profits.

Who really pays the profits tax? After all, corporations are not people; ultimately every tax dollar must be paid by a real person. The simplest view is that shareholders pay the tax. Many tax experts question this simple view, for reasons that are insanely technical; the debate over the true incidence of the profits tax has generated a vast, thoroughly confusing academic literature.

Fortunately, big cuts in corporate profits taxes are not currently on the table. If they do arrive, we'll have to worry about who would really benefit. But for now, we have the luxury of ignoring that difficult question.

The estate tax. The estate tax—a tax on the value of someone's estate after he or she dies—is not comparable to the three big taxes we've just described in terms of the revenue it collects. This year it is expected to yield only $35 billion. However, while Bush only wants to *reduce* the income tax, he wants to *eliminate* the estate tax. This gives the estate tax disproportionate importance in his plan: when the plan is fully phased in, the elimination of the estate tax will account for almost a quarter of the total tax reduction.

The important thing to understand about the estate tax is that it is a tax primarily on the very, very rich. This is in part because wealth is much more unequally distributed than income: the wealthiest 1 percent of families owns close to half the nation's assets. It is also because the estate tax itself is sharply progressive: individual estates under $675,000 are not taxed at all, and the exemption is twice that for married couples; under current law that exemption is scheduled to rise to $1 million for each member of a couple by 2006.

Because of the size of the exemption, only about 2 percent of estates pay any estate tax, and most of those estates pay very little. In fact, in 1997 almost half of the estate tax was paid by only 2400 estates, with a *minimum* value of $5 million. About 2.3 million people died that year, so nearly half the estate tax was paid by only the biggest 0.1 percent of the estates.

There's a lot of mythology surrounding the estate tax; proponents of estate tax repeal often portray it as a major burden on family-owned businesses or farms. This turns out to be another urban legend. Only a few percent of the estates that pay taxes include a family business. Furthermore, the existing law gives family businesses and farms special treatment: the exemption is doubled when a business or farm constitutes a large share of the property, and the law also allows inheritors of such businesses to defer the tax payment for up to 14 years. Real-life cases of small businesses or family farms that must be sold to pay estate taxes are very rare.

That, then, is the broad outline of the federal tax system. The taxes we've just described, together with a grab bag of taxes on gasoline, alcohol, imported trucks, and more, collected approximately $2 trillion last year. What did your government do with the money?

Putting It Out: Where the Money Goes

About 11 percent of the federal budget goes to pay interest on the national debt. How do we think about the rest of it?

One useful way to think about government spending is to divide it into three roughly defined categories. First, there are "public goods": government programs that in principle benefit everyone and are not allocated to particular individuals. The big-ticket item here is the defense budget, which is slightly less than 20 percent of federal spending, excluding paying interest on the national debt. But the court system, the air traffic control system, the interstate highway system, and foreign aid all fall into that category.

Second, there is "social insurance": programs that are intended to protect middle-class people from some of the vicissitudes of life. The big social insurance programs are Social Security and Medicare, but the category also includes smaller programs like unemployment insurance. In 1995, the last year for which there is an official estimate, social insurance accounted for about 45 percent of federal spending other than interest payments.

Finally, there is "public aid": programs that are designed to help the poor or the otherwise unfortunate. The line between social insurance and public aid is a bit blurry, but a rough distinction is between programs that are "means-tested"—that require recipients to show that they are sufficiently poor—and those that are not. Means-tested programs account for about 13 percent of federal non-interest spending. The biggest item is Medicaid, which provides medical care for the poor; other items include food stamps and the Earned Income Tax Credit, which supplements the wages of poor workers.

If you want a picture of the federal government, then, think of it as an enterprise with three divisions. One division handles defense and other public goods; one handles middle-class insurance programs, mainly Social Security and Medicare; one helps the poor with Medicaid and food stamps.

It's always helpful when listening to politicians to keep this picture in mind. When politicians say that they want a smaller government, don't just nod your head: ask yourself (and if possible ask them) which of these three divisions they propose to shrink. Remember that while there is plenty of waste and fraud in the federal government, this is true of any large organization, including private corporations. (Read *Dilbert* if you don't believe me.) So it isn't realistic for politicians to claim that they can shrink the government to any noticeable extent without giving up some services that the government currently provides. If they want a smaller government, what do they propose to eliminate?

For what it's worth, two of the three divisions of the federal enterprise have been under pressure to cut spending for many years. Public goods spending is down dramatically as a share of the budget. Mainly that's because the end of the Cold War led to a large decrease in military spending, but everything from foreign aid to NASA has faced budget austerity even as the private economy boomed. With the exception of Medicaid, means-tested programs have also faced austerity; remember that it was during the Clinton years that we ended welfare as we knew it.

The growth sector of the federal budget—now, and even more in the decade ahead—is in the area of middle-class social insurance. And in the United States that usually means programs for retirees.

The Retirement State

As he was leaving office, Dwight Eisenhower famously warned against the power of the "military-industrial complex." And his warning made a lot of sense at the time: America's government during his administration was largely a military state, with defense accounting for well over half of non-interest spending.

But in the year 2001 the military state is long gone. What has replaced it? A retirement state. To caricature things a bit, but in a way that captures the essence, the federal government has become a large retirement program that does some military stuff and a bit of humanitarian stuff on the side.

Right now the two big federal programs explicitly aimed at retirees—Social Security and Medicare—account for about 40 percent of total spending other than paying interest on the national debt. And that's not the whole story: if you include retirement benefits for federal workers, benefits for veterans, and the large share of Medicaid that goes to the elderly poor, you find that about half of non-interest federal spending—and more than 60 percent of non-defense non-interest federal spending—goes to provide benefits to people over age 65. This share will grow even larger starting in 2011, the year in which the oldest members of the baby boom generation will reach retirement age.

We'll see in the next three chapters that the central role of retirees in the federal budget makes a huge difference to the way you should think about our budget surplus. But for now let me ask how the importance of programs oriented at retirees should affect our views about whether the U.S. government is too big.

There isn't much room for shrinking the other two divisions of our government. Our military complains that it is already too small to handle the jobs of peacekeeping in a world where the United States has no major military rivals; if the world changes, demands on the military can only increase. Meanwhile, our public aid programs are by far the least generous of any advanced nation; how much less generous can we get?

So you can't propose to shrink the federal government significantly without in effect proposing to reduce benefits to retirees. And while politicians rarely admit their desire to shrink those middle-class retirement programs—when Newt Gingrich declared in 1995 that "we didn't get rid of [Medicare] in round one because we don't think that that's politically smart," he was not being, well, politically smart—others have been more honest. In 1998 *The New Republic* summed it up when it ran a cover with the headline "Greedy Geezers."

So should we try to make government smaller by spending less on programs for the elderly? Ultimately that's a question with no right answer; it's a value judgment. But let me offer my own reasons for thinking that our retirement programs, expensive as they are, are worth the cost.

It comes down to this: Social Security and Medicare have made a big positive difference to the lives of the less-well-off elderly. Once upon a time desperate poverty among the elderly in this country was alarmingly common; as late as the 1950s, elderly Americans were far more likely to be below the poverty line than the population at large. Now, thanks largely to Social Security, they are far *less* likely to be poor than the average; that represents a dramatic reduction in misery, one that seems to be worth even its high price. Nowadays *children* live disproportionately in poverty. You should bear this in mind if you think that we spend too much on public aid.

Meanwhile, Medicare makes a big difference not only to the poor but also to the middle-income elderly. Since Medicare was introduced in the mid-1960s, there has been a revolution in medical care for the elderly: procedures that were rare or nonexistent 35 years ago, like hip replacements and heart bypass operations, have become commonplace. But these procedures are expensive. Were it not for Medicare, they would be affordable only for a well-off minority of older Americans. And that would make our society a lot more unequal than it is, in a sense that goes beyond dollars and cents.

In a widely circulated essay, the conservative writer Irving Kristol has argued that in our affluent society income inequality is irrelevant, because it is swamped by "social equality." "In all our major cities," he declared, "there is not a single restaurant where a CEO can lunch or dine with the absolute assurance that he will not run into his secretary. . . . Only experts can deduce a person's economic status from his clothing; who doesn't wear blue jeans these days?"

But what if we were a society in which an elderly person who has hip trouble gets a hip replacement if he or she is rich, but becomes a cripple if he or she is not? What if clogged arteries meant a bypass operation if you were rich, death if you weren't? That sounds like a pretty serious case of social inequality to me.

Medicare is a large part of the reason why we mostly aren't that kind of society. It's a very expensive program, and it will become more expensive as medical science advances. But I think that it is a price well worth paying.

So should we really complain about "greedy geezers"? The main complaint one can make about Social Security and Medicare is that they aren't means-tested: they provide full benefits even to people who would be in fine shape without them. Perhaps one could say that affluent beneficiaries of the retirement state are a bit greedy. But overall, the retirement state has made us a kinder, gentler, and, in my opinion, morally better nation.

4

THE FROG WHO TURNED INTO A PRINCE

ORIGINS OF THE SURPLUS

O NCE UPON A TIME, not all that long ago, the federal budget was like a loathsome frog. From 1970 to 1998 the budget was consistently in the red. The numbers were small at first, except during recession years; but when Ronald Reagan simultaneously cut taxes and increased military spending, the deficit exploded. In 1986, even though a growing economy was boosting tax receipts, the deficit reached an astonishing 5 percent of GDP. For comparison, right now investors are fleeing Argentina because they fear that its budget deficit of less than 3 percent of GDP is a harbinger of eventual fiscal collapse.

Investors, of course, never lost faith in the solvency of the U.S. government; they always thought that somehow, someday, the frog would turn into a prince. And their faith was justified:

that huge deficit 15 years ago has become an impressive surplus today. But will today's black ink fade as quickly as yesterday's red ink?

A first step in answering that question is to ask how we moved from deficit to surplus. What were the sources of the big turnaround?

Payrolling Our Dues: Social Security and the Surplus

In 1983, just two years after Ronald Reagan pushed a huge cut in income taxes through Congress, that same Congress passed a substantial tax *increase*. But it wasn't the income tax that went up, it was the payroll tax. That almost forgotten tax increase is responsible for much of our current budget surplus, but the reasons behind that tax increase also explain why much of today's surplus isn't really a surplus. This may sound a bit cryptic, but it will make sense once we look at how the Social Security system, which along with Medicare is funded by the payroll tax, actually works.

On the face of it, Social Security looks like an ordinary pension plan: you contribute part of your paycheck all your working life, then you draw a pension after you retire. But an ordinary pension fund is actually "funded": your contributions are invested in stocks or bonds, and those investments are what make it possible for the plan to pay benefits when you retire. Social Security, by contrast, has traditionally been run on a "pay-as-you-go" basis: the money you pay in is immediately paid out to today's retirees, and when you retire your pension will be paid out of taxes on younger workers. This system was modified a bit in 1983—that's what the payroll tax increase was about—but the assets of the Social Security system remain far less (about $9 trillion less) than what would be needed if it were to be "fully funded" like an ordinary pension plan.

All this can seem a bit confusing; economists who work in this area find it helpful to think in terms of a simplified parable, known in the jargon as the "overlapping-generations model."

Imagine a country in which people's lives can be divided into two equal periods. There are no children in this world, just workers (people in the first period of their lives) and retirees (people in the second period). In the absence of a Social Security system, retirees would have to live off their savings from their working years.

Now introduce a Social Security system. This system imposes a tax each period on young, working people and pays out the proceeds of that tax in the same period to older, retired people. And it does this period after period.

This system is a terrific deal for the first generation of retirees. They have not paid in, yet they get retirement benefits, paid for by taxes imposed on the next generation.

After that, the deal will not seem quite so terrific. Each generation will make contributions during its working years, then receive benefits during its retirement years. So it will look to the participants like an ordinary pension plan. But it isn't: it's a pay-as-you-go system in which the money each generation puts in isn't invested, but is simply paid out to current retirees.

That doesn't mean that workers get no return on the money they have put into the system. As long as the size of the working population and the average wage rate are rising, each generation will contribute more to the system than the generation before. Since what each generation receives is what the next generation pays in, each generation gets more than what it put in—that is, it gets a positive rate of return on its contributions. Nonetheless, that return may be less than what workers could have earned by investing their money in stocks or bonds. A politician trying to change the system might use that difference between market returns and the apparent "return" on Social Security accounts as an argument for replacing the pay-as-you-go system with private accounts. And of course that's exactly the argument Bush made during the campaign. We'll see in a minute, however, that the comparison is bogus, and that privatization is a lot harder than it sounds.

Taking the system as given, it seems as if it could run forever. Each generation would support the retirement of the generation before, and everyone would live (and die) happily ever after—unless something goes wrong.

What could go wrong? The system offers a reasonable deal as long as each generation is bigger and richer than the generation before. But if economic growth should slow and, worse yet, if the birth rate should drop, we would have a serious problem. Suppose that a big generation were to be followed by a small one. When the big generation retired, there would be relatively few workers paying in and a lot of retirees drawing benefits. Something would have to give: benefits would have to be cut, taxes increased, or both.

And sure enough, that's what happened. The American baby boom was followed by a baby bust; by 1983 it was already clear that when the baby boomers reached retirement age—which will start to happen in 2011—there would an unprecedented number of retirees per active worker. Current demographic projections say that while right now there are 3.2 Americans of working age for every American 65 or older, by 2030 there will be only 2. The nation as a whole will have the age distribution of Florida today. If Social Security were to be run on its traditional pay-as-you-go basis, working-age Americans would stagger under the burden of caring for their elders.

Luckily, such things don't happen suddenly; the demographic deluge that will begin in 2011 was already clearly visible in 1983. Even more luckily, in that year Congress chose to accept the recommendations of a commission headed by none other than Alan Greenspan that included an increase in the payroll tax.

The effect of that tax increase was that the Social Security system began, for the first time, to accumulate large amounts of money in its "trust fund." According to current estimates, by the time the baby boomers start to retire there will be about $3 trillion in the pot. The money in that pot will earn interest, so much interest that for a number of years after the magic date of 2011 the system will still be in surplus, and the pot of money will continue to grow. If tax rates are not raised and benefits are not cut, however, demography will finally dominate: eventually the cost of paying benefits to a growing older population will exceed both tax revenues and interest earnings; according to current projections this will happen in around 2025. At that point the system will have to start dipping into its reserves, eventually running out, again according to current projections, in 2038. But because of that 1983 move to increase payroll taxes, what would have been an imminent crisis has been pushed far off into the future.

One way to think about what the Greenspan commission did is to say that it moved the Social Security system part of the way toward being a real pension fund—one that actually holds enough assets to pay for the benefits it promises. But the move went only part way—and this has been a source of confusion, much of it deliberate.

It's Your Money—Or Is It?

This book is about taxes, not about proposals for Social Security reform. But because the interpretation of the budget surplus and the problems of Social Security are closely related, we need to take a brief detour here to talk about some common misunderstandings about Social Security—misunderstandings that candidate Bush, alas, did his best to spread during the campaign.

Go back for a moment to our simplified parable about Social Security in an "overlapping-generations" world. In that world, as we've already seen, Social Security would *look* to each individual like an ordinary pension plan. But as we also saw, it might seem to be a pension plan that does not offer a particularly good return. And in the real world, today's young workers can expect a real rate of return (a return after inflation) on their Social Security contributions of only about 2 percent. That compares with a real rate of return on government bonds of about 4 percent, and a historical real rate of return on stocks of about 8 percent (though since stock prices are now much higher relative to earnings than they used to be, there are reasons to believe that future returns on stocks will be lower than they were in the past).

So wouldn't workers be better off opting out of Social Security and investing the money for themselves? That's the notion that Bush spread during the campaign, with his insistent declaration that "it's your money." And despite the best efforts of people who knew better to explain why this was a bogus notion, most reports in the news media never made clear what was wrong with Bush's claim.

What *was* wrong with it? Think about the parable. In any given period benefits to the older generation must be paid out of the taxes collected from the younger generation, who will then receive benefits paid by the next generation, and so on. Now suppose that the younger generation were to opt out of the system and invest their money themselves. Who would pay the benefits to today's retirees?

Remember that the Social Security contributions of the older generation went to support the generation before; they accepted this, because they were in effect promised that today's working-age population would support them in turn. So the system has an *implicit debt* to retirees (and more generally to those who have already paid in considerable amounts, like middle-aged baby boomers). It makes no sense to talk about how much people could earn by withdrawing from Social Security and investing their own money without explaining first who is going pay the system's implicit debt.

And that implicit debt is very, very large—much larger than the explicit debt of the entire federal government. A rough estimate is that in order to turn Social Security into a "fully funded" system—one that is like a pension fund, in which you could really say that "it's your money"—we would need to add about $10 trillion to the trust fund.

Where did that $10 trillion debt come from? Basically from the generous returns given to early recipients of Social Security benefits, who, like the first generation in the parable, got a lot in return for small contributions. And the reason why the implicit returns on Social Security contributions right now are low is not that the system wastes your money; it is that part of your contributions must in effect go to make interest payments on that huge but hidden debt.

All of this would have been much clearer, much more obvious to voters, if the Social Security system were still being run on a purely pay-as-you-go basis. But because of the payroll tax increase in the 1980s, the system is now acting in part as a true pension fund—which makes it easier for a politician to proclaim that Social Security contributions are "your money" and that you should be getting a higher return. As they say, no good deed goes unpunished. The important point is that Social Security is still mainly unfunded and that the surpluses it will be running over the next decade are not money available to finance other projects, such as tax cuts or, for that matter, the creation of private investment accounts. That's what I meant when I said that the Social Security surplus is not a true surplus.

And there's one other important point: because the Social Security system has a huge implicit debt, when we talk about "paying off the national debt" we are telling the literal truth but missing the larger point. Even if the federal government were to pay off all its explicit debt, it would still be $10 trillion in the red because of the Social Security system's implicit debt. It sounds like a paradox, but it's true. As we'll see in Chapter 6, this makes a huge difference when you ask how we should run our budget.

The Big Squeeze: How Spending Got Smaller

The Social Security system started running big surpluses in the late 1980s. Nonetheless, until just two years ago those surpluses were a bit of a joke, because they were more than offset by deficits on the part of the rest of the government. Social Security and Medicare (I'll discuss Medicare in Chapter 6) were taking in more from the payroll tax than they were spending, but the rest of the government—the "on-budget" government—was spending more than it took in from other taxes. So the Social Security surplus was a matter of putting money into the government's left pocket even as a larger sum was being extracted from the right pocket.

Now, however, the rest of the government has also moved into surplus. In fiscal 2001 the government's overall surplus is expected to be $280 billion; more than half of this will come from the combined Social Security and Medicare surpluses, but there remains a substantial surplus in the rest of the budget. How did that happen?

The short answer is that spending was squeezed while the tax take soared. Let's look at each of these in turn.

Budget experts typically divide spending into two parts: "entitlements" and "discretionary" spending. Social Security and Medicare are entitlements: the law specifies how much a retiree is entitled to receive, which medical procedures he or she is entitled to have the government pay for, and so on. Entitlements are not engraved in stone; the law can always be changed. But politicians know that they revise entitlements at their peril, so this part of the budget tends to be relatively if not absolutely immovable.

Discretionary spending, by contrast, is much more a matter of, well, discretion. Should Congress approve a new weapons system, a new program of aid to schools, etc.? Such decisions are made every year. So most of the action in budgeting focuses on the discretionary items.

A large part of the story of our surplus is that discretionary spending fell sharply as a share both of federal spending and of the economy as a whole. In 1986 discretionary spending was 9.5 percent of GDP; in 2001 it was only 6 percent.

Incidentally, when people talk about "big government" they generally have in mind discretionary spending, not entitlements. So it's worth noticing that in that sense government has actually gotten a lot *smaller* relative to the economy over the past 15 years.

Most of that shrinkage was due to the end of the Cold War. Defense spending was 6.2 percent of GDP in 1986, but only 2.9 percent in 2001. But non-defense discretionary spending also grew more slowly than the economy, falling from 3.3 to 3.1 percent of GDP. Again, if you think that we suffer from a severe case of "big government" you should be aware that even civilian discretionary spending is lower today as a share of the economy than it has been since Dwight Eisenhower—yes, Eisenhower—was president.

What lay behind this spending restraint? Fear of deficits helped keep a lid on spending proposals. But probably the most important ingredient in the political recipe was divided government: for all but two of those 15 years, the White House and the Congress were controlled by different parties. This meant that neither could easily push through pet projects.

The Revenue Boom

The other side of the great move into surplus was a surge in revenues. In the second half of the 1990s money began pouring into federal coffers at a rate that made earlier, pessimistic budget forecasts look foolish. What happened?

A large part of the answer was a takeoff in economic growth. Economic growth averaged less than 3 percent per year from 1973 until 1995, but then—probably because of the way new technology enhanced productivity—it accelerated to an average of more than 4 percent over the next five years. A bigger economy means more income subject to taxes, so the economic boom naturally translated into a revenue boom.

But that wasn't the whole story: revenue grew even faster than the economy. Indeed, as conservatives never tire of pointing out, the overall tax take of the federal government is a higher percentage of GDP than ever before. Some of that is because of the increase in the payroll tax, but revenue from income taxes and profit taxes has also grown considerably faster than the economy as a whole.

So did tax rates go up? Yes and no. Income taxes were increased both under the elder Bush and under Clinton. Even so, the tax rate at any given level of income remains far below what it was before Ronald Reagan. The main explanation of a rising tax take was a change in the distribution of national income.

First, profits grew faster than wages; since profits are taxed more heavily than ordinary workers' wages, that increased revenue.

Second, incomes grew much more rapidly at the top than at the bottom of the income distribution. I've already mentioned this effect. Remember that the income tax is the main tax on the top fifth of taxpayers and, correspondingly, that most of the tax is paid by families in the top fifth of the distribution.

Between 1986 and 1999 average family income rose by 18 percent, but income among the top fifth rose 28 percent; income among the top 5 percent rose 46 percent, and income among the top one percent probably doubled. So income growth was concentrated among families in the highest tax brackets, thus pushing up revenues more rapidly than average income growth.

Third, the great stock market boom, which doubled the Dow and quadrupled the Nasdaq over five years, meant that virtually anyone who sold a stock after 1995 sold it for a big gain—and capital gains are taxable. The result was a further boost to tax revenues.

The Bottom Line

So how did the huge deficits of the 1980s turn into the large surpluses of the millennium? The answer is a bit of everything. There was brave, foresighted behavior: the payroll tax increase of 1983, the income tax increase of 1993, and, yes, the elder Bush's politically disastrous decision to break his campaign pledge and raise taxes. There was spending austerity, grounded less in principle than in political deadlock. And there was a large element of luck: not only did the economy experience an unexpected boom, but the way the boom played out just happened to be especially helpful to federal finances.

The big question now is whether the prince will stay princely and handsome, or whether he will turn back into a frog. What is the outlook for the federal budget in the years ahead?

5

BIRDS IN THE
BUSH

PROJECTING THE SURPLUS

N THE FISCAL year that will end September 2001, the federal budget surplus is expected to be more than $280 billion—a remarkable turnaround from the deficits of the past, even if more than half of it comes from the necessary surpluses of Social Security and Medicare. You might think that this surplus would be enough to pay for the plans of politicians.

But no: the debate over tax cuts has been framed not in terms of this year's or even next year's surplus but in terms of projected surpluses over the next decade, and in particular the Congressional Budget Office projection of a $5.6 trillion surplus over that period. Rather than focus on the rather impressive bird in hand, we are counting on a couple of dozen birds that are still in the bush.

This focus on a ten-year surplus is extremely unfortunate, because ten years turns out to be pessimal (the opposite of optimal) as a planning horizon. On one hand it's too long: realistically, nobody has a good idea of what the economy or the budget will look like a decade from now. On the other hand, if you feel that you must try to make guesses about the long run, ten years is too short. In particular, it means that we will be averting our eyes from the way the budget will look after the baby boomers reach retirement age, a process that will begin in earnest eleven years from now.

If I thought I could get away with it, I would just refuse to discuss tax cut plans in terms of the ten-year prospect. But because this is the way everyone talks about it, it can't be avoided.

How to Interpret Those Projections

You might think that the biggest source of controversy when it comes to budget projections involves the uncertainties of economic forecasting. And these uncertainties are certainly very large. If the annual growth rate of the U.S. economy is even a few tenths of a percentage point more or less than the Congressional Budget Office currently assumes in its projections, that alone could make its ten-year surplus projection wrong by a trillion dollars or more. Other economic uncertainties are equally severe: given the large and growing importance of Medicare and Medicaid in the federal budget, an acceleration of the trend in medical costs—which seems to be happening—could wreak havoc with projections of government outlays.

But as it turns out, the biggest source of controversy involves not the economic assumptions but the entire meaning of the CBO's projection.

What does it mean when the Congressional Budget Office "projects" a surplus of $5.6 trillion over the next ten years? It doesn't mean that we will actually run that surplus, even if the economic assumptions turn out to be exactly on target. After all, Congress will surely pass new programs, perhaps eliminate old programs, and will do *something* to taxes. Since the CBO isn't in the business of political forecasting, its projection doesn't try to anticipate what politicians will do in the future.

Instead, the projection is written in the subjunctive: it is an estimate of what the surplus would be, given likely economic trends, *if policies were to remain unchanged.* That is, it is supposed to be an estimate of what would happen if the government not only left the tax law alone but also kept everything else where it is—the same size military, the same level of unemployment benefits, and so on. Or, as it is sometimes stated, the projection is an estimate of what the surplus would be under "current policy."

"Current policy" is relatively easy to define when it comes to revenue projections: you can predict how much revenue would come in if current tax law remained in effect. Now, one needs to make a choice between strict legalism and realism here. Congress has in the past granted some tax breaks that are supposedly temporary, and will soon expire, but that are almost certain to be renewed. And there is one big problem with existing tax law, involving something called the alternative minimum tax (more about that later), which will surely require a change in the law regardless of how the current debate plays out. Most budget experts believe that a realistic definition of "current policy" would actually reflect these predictable actions, rather than assuming no new tax legislation. According to an invaluable study by Alan Auerbach of the University of California, Berkeley, and William Gale of the Brookings Institution, a more realistic treatment of expiring tax provisions and of the alternative minimum tax would shave more than $200 billion off the CBO's surplus projection. Still, defining current policy on taxes is relatively straightforward.

Defining current policy on entitlements, mainly Social Security and Medicare, is also fairly straightforward. We know what the law says retirees are entitled to receive; so if you can make economic projections about items like health care costs (a very big if), you can make a spending projection based on the assumption that the law remains unchanged.

Where it really gets tricky is in defining current policy for the rest of government spending—that is, the discretionary part of the budget. And that is where the CBO projections have come in for the greatest criticism.

A Peculiar Definition of Unchanged Policy

Of that $5.6 trillion surplus projection, a little more than half—$2.9 trillion—consists of the surpluses that the CBO expects the Social Security and Medicare systems to run. (Medicare is running a surplus for the same reason that Social Security is—as a program that receives money from workers and pays benefits to retirees, it is trying to make provisions for the coming wave of retiring baby boomers.) As we've seen, those surpluses are in a fundamental sense not really surpluses, because they are necessary preparations for the coming demographic deluge. But while nobody doubts that the CBO forecast there will turn out to be wrong, not many experts have asserted that it is strongly biased one way or the other.

The rest of the projection, however, is a different matter. Here the CBO's notion of current policy looks to outside observers, myself included, like a radical downsizing of government over the next decade. This might happen, though it seems unlikely; the point is that the CBO is supposed to project what would happen if the federal government continues to do more or less what it does now, not to build in a radical policy change.

The way the CBO defines "maintaining current policy" is to assume that there is *no change in real discretionary spending*. That is, it assumes that keeping the role of government unchanged would mean keeping the number of dollars spent on things other than Social Security and Medicare unchanged after adjusting for inflation.

To see why this is an unreasonable way to define current policy, consider one example of a government program: air traffic control. Suppose that the federal government were to keep real spending on air traffic control constant for the next ten years, so that the number of controllers and the capacity of the radar systems stayed the same for a decade. Would that *feel* like no change in policy, like a government whose role in the economy had not changed?

Of course not. It would feel like a drastic cut in government services, because the same number of air traffic controllers would have to manage a greatly increased volume of air traffic. And air traffic is not a special case: just about everything that the government deals with will require more resources in order to maintain the current level of government services, because we are a growing country with a growing economy. (And when it comes to defense spending, our potential adversaries are also growing countries with growing economies.)

Even a highly conservative definition of maintaining current policy would be one under which real spending *per capita* remains unchanged. The U.S. population is expected to grow about 10 percent over the next decade, so the CBO's projection assumes a 10 percent *decline* in real per capita spending. Many economists would go further and argue that a truly reasonable definition of unchanged policy would be one in which spending remained constant as a percentage of GDP; by contrast, the CBO projection assumes a 25 percent decline in that percentage.

And even these comparisons understate how unrealistic the CBO's definition of maintaining current policy really is. We can be sure that some parts of discretionary spending—defense in particular—won't be cut per capita, and probably won't even fall as a percentage of GDP. Defense is half of discretionary spending; if the defense share of GDP remains constant, the CBO projection would imply a 50 percent decline in civilian spending as a percentage of GDP. And bear in mind that civilian discretionary spending is no higher a share of the economy today than it was 40 years ago.

The important, and obvious, point is that the CBO's projection isn't a description of what the budget surplus would be under current policy. It's a projection of what the budget surplus would be if government programs were radically cut, to levels not seen since the 1950s or earlier. That may be what some politicians want, but it is not the way the projections are being interpreted by the public. Instead, the CBO surplus projection is being seen as telling us how much we can cut taxes *without* either going into deficit or making drastic cutbacks in government services. And it just doesn't do that.

So that $2.7 trillion supposedly available outside Social Security and Medicare is too large a number. Auerbach and Gale estimate that correcting the CBO projection to assume constant spending *per capita* would subtract $400 billion off that number; correcting it to assume constant spending as a share of GDP would subtract another $600 billion.

Even if we accept the CBO's revenue forecasts, the surplus projection should be considerably lower than the number it uses. But should we accept the revenue forecast?

Capital Gains and Capitol Games

Let's admit that the CBO revenue projections could turn out to be too pessimistic. Those projections assume a rate of economic growth over the next ten years that is only a bit faster than the rate we actually achieved over the last decade; since growth accelerated in the second half of the last decade, that is considerably lower than the rates we have become accustomed to in recent years. If it turns out that the economic boom of the second half of the 1990s continues through the next decade, and if the economy grows at an annual rate of 4 percent, tax collections by the end of the decade will be quite a lot higher than forecast, and the CBO's projections will turn out to have been excessively pessimistic. On the other hand, if the "new economy" turns out to have been a sprinter rather than a marathon runner, the CBO's projections of revenue will turn out to be greatly exaggerated. And nobody knows which story is right.

But there are other reasons to believe that the CBO projections of revenue for any given rate of economic growth are unreasonably high. One set of reasons is agonizingly technical, but it comes back to the tricky question of what it means to talk about maintaining current policy. On taxes, the CBO takes an approach of strict literalism: it assumes that no new tax laws will be passed—including laws that simply renew tax provisions that have been renewed repeatedly in the past. In effect, it assumes no *de jure* change—no change in the letter of the law. But it's much more sensible to think that current policy means no *de facto* change—that the spirit of the tax law, as it currently stands, will be maintained. In the past, expiring tax breaks have been renewed; if you make the more sensible assumption that Congress will do the same in the future, the predicted tax receipts will go down. This is not a huge item: $80 billion, according to Auerbach and Gale. But $80 billion here, $80 billion there, and soon you're talking about real money.

More important, the CBO assumes that a hitherto obscure aspect of the tax code, the alternative minimum tax (AMT), will be left unchanged even as it starts to apply to many more taxpayers. This tax was originally intended as a way to prevent high-income taxpayers from claiming an excessive number of deductions: if a taxpayer's deductions are too large according to a complicated formula, the regular tax table is thrown out and the alternative minimum tax applies instead. In practice, the AMT typically falls not on the very rich but on upper-middle-class taxpayers who claim large deductions for some reason. (I know an academic who took a leave from his post to work temporarily in a lower-paid public service job; his deduction for the property taxes on his home triggered the alternative minimum tax.)

People who find themselves paying the alternative minimum tax are generally furious, but there aren't many such tax-payers—yet. Only about 1.5 percent of the population currently pays this tax. But because the criteria under which the tax applies are stated in dollar terms—that is, they are not adjusted for rises in the cost of living—the AMT will, even under current policy, start to affect more taxpayers. Current estimates suggest that under current law, by 2010 about 15 percent of taxpayers will be paying the AMT.

We can safely predict that this is not going to happen; there is no question that Congress will, one way or another, adjust the AMT to prevent it from becoming so widespread a burden. But any such adjustment will reduce revenues compared with the CBO projections; Auerbach and Gale estimate that an AMT adjustment would reduce the budget surplus by $130 billion.

As we'll see in Chapter 7, the AMT will become an even bigger issue if the Bush tax cut is passed in anything like its current form. Indeed, it is one of the major reasons to regard the administration's claims that its plans are affordable as implausible.

Aside from these technical concerns over expiring provisions and the AMT, there is one more major reason to think that the CBO's revenue projections are too high: the high tax take in recent years has had a lot to do with the bull market on Wall Street. And that, in case you hadn't noticed, has gone away.

Between 1994 and 2000 annual federal revenue from taxes on capital gains increased by $70 billion. That's a big number compared with the projected budget surplus; if capital gains taxes were to drop back to their levels of the early 1990s, the surplus over the next decade could fall by close to a trillion dollars.

Now, the CBO projection does assume that the revenue from capital gains taxes will taper off during the decade ahead—but that it will remain at levels that are very high by historical standards. In light of the market's plunge, that does not seem like a safe, or even a reasonable, assumption.

Educated Guesses

We really are talking about fuzzy math here. Could it turn out that over the next decade the federal government runs a surplus of $8 trillion? Yes, it could happen. Could it turn out that the surplus is only $2 trillion? Yes, that could happen too.

But complete agnosticism about the future is not an option; some sort of guess has to be hazarded.

Table 2 shows the revision of the CBO projection suggested by Auerbach and Gale. Even if you take a very conservative view of what it means to maintain current policy—keeping the tax system unchanged *de facto* as opposed to *de jure*, and keeping real spending per capita constant—the surplus projection drops to $4.9 trillion. If you make the more realistic assumption that current policy means keeping spending as a per-

Table 2

THE TEN-YEAR SURPLUS: THE CBO PROJECTION AND SOME ADJUSTMENTS ($ TRILLION)	
Congressional Budget Office projection:	$5.610
Reduce by:	
Expiring provisions	$0.082
Alternative minimum tax fix	$0.130
Keeping real discretionary spending per capita constant	$0.481
Maximum reasonable budget projection:	$ 4.917
If discretionary spending as percent of GDP constant:	$4.280

Source: Alan Auerbach and William Gale, "Tax cuts and the budget," Brookings Institution, March 2001.

centage of GDP unchanged, the projection drops to $4.3 trillion.

I am personally even more downbeat than Auerbach and Gale, because I think that the CBO is overestimating likely capital gains taxes. I would argue that a reasonable surplus projection under current policy is actually below $4 trillion.

But we're still talking about a big surplus. Shouldn't the government do something with that surplus, including cutting taxes? No, not necessarily; in the next chapter we'll see why.

6

TAKING TOO MUCH?

SETTING A SURPLUS TARGET

ONE OF GEORGE W. BUSH'S favorite remarks on the campaign trail was to declare that a budget surplus means that the government is taking too much of your money. And there is a sense in which he was right: a government that ran a budget surplus forever would be acting very peculiarly.

But of course no government would or could run a surplus forever. Sooner or later, one way or another, budget surpluses end. And if Bush meant to say that governments should *never* run a surplus, that any surplus any time is a sign that the government is taking too much—well, in that case he was just wrong. There are times when governments should run surpluses; this is one of those times.

The question is not whether the federal government should

be running a surplus right now, but how big that surplus should be. To answer that question we need to back up a bit and look at some general economic principles, then come back to our current situation.

Steady as You Go: Budgeting for the Long Run

The basic principle of sound long-run tax policy is very simple: the government should try to find a tax rate that works for the long run and stick to it. That is, the government should avoid moving tax rates up and down over time. A steady tax rate of 20 percent is better than a rate that is sometimes 10 percent, sometimes 30 percent, even if the average tax rate over time is the same.

The main reason why steady as you go is better is that the economic cost of taxes—the drag on the economy I discussed in Chapter 2—rises much more than in proportion to the actual tax rate. This means that the losses a government inflicts on the economy when it raises the tax rate from 20 to 30 percent are bigger than the gains when it cuts the rate from 20 to 10. So a rate that remains steady at 20 will do less harm than one that bounces between 10 and 30.

Fluctuating tax rates also offer an incentive to "time-shift" economic activities: to try to arrange your taxable actions so that they occur in low-tax years rather than in high-tax years. This is a further costly distortion of economic incentives that can be avoided by keeping tax rates more or less level over time.

But while there are good reasons to keep taxes more or less level from year to year, there are also good reasons why government spending is *not* the same from year to year. Sometimes there are extraordinary expenses—of which the most important historically has been war. How do you reconcile the goal of steady taxes with the need to vary spending? The answer is that during "bad" years, when there are exceptional spending needs, the government should run a budget deficit; during "good" years the government should save for the future by running surpluses.

In the past, "bad" and "good" basically meant war and peace. Responsible governments like that of the United States or the United Kingdom ran budget deficits in wartime, running up large debts, then paid off those debts during peacetime. Even now that is hardly an irrelevant criterion. The United States is currently in the extraordinary position of having no serious military rivals, standing alone as the world's only superpower. This won't last forever—such things never do—so even on traditional grounds this would be a good time to run budget surpluses.

But of course nowadays we aren't mainly a military state; we're mainly a retirement state. And that's the main reason why the U.S. government should be running budget surpluses.

Demography and Destiny

These are the best of times for the federal budget. We're at peace; but more important, my g-g-generation is still in the prime of life, working, earning, paying taxes, and *not* collecting Social Security benefits or sending Medicare our medical bills—yet.

A large budget surplus is appropriate and prudent for America right now because we know that things are going to get worse, since the age distribution of the population is going to get much less favorable for the federal budget. We are basically in the position of a healthy middle-aged couple, in our late 40s or early 50s, at the peak of our earning power. Would a couple in that position feel that it was acting responsibly as long as its spending was no greater than its income? Certainly not: the couple ought to be saving for its retirement. And the federal government similarly should be saving for the retirement of the baby boomers.

How much should we be saving? That is, how large should the budget surplus be? One thing is for sure: the minimum prudent federal surplus over the next decade is $3.3 trillion.

Why $3.3 trillion? This is a projection of the combined surplus that will be run by all of the federal government's retirement trust funds. I've already talked at length about Social Security, which is the biggest of those funds; but it's not the whole story. There's also Medicare, which like Social Security is a program for retirees, and which is currently running surpluses for the same reason. And finally—something that is usually ignored, but which should be considered in the same class—there are federal pension funds that owe benefits to both military and civilian retirees. (Auerbach and Gale have been on a lonely crusade to get the federal government to adopt responsible pension budgeting for these funds—something that the law requires of private corporations.)

Why should the overall surplus be no less than the combined surplus of the trust funds? Or to use the Washington jargon, why should we put those trust fund surpluses in a "lockbox"? First, we know that the projected surpluses in Social Security and Medicare, though enough to postpone the eventual crises in the two systems, are not enough to put off those crises indefinitely. Medicare, in particular, will run out of money sometime before 2020. So even taking the Social Security and Medicare systems as they are, extending their life would require some additional "topping up" from the rest of the federal budget.

Second, there is a good case for reforming Social Security—turning it into something closer to a true, fully funded pension system for the middle class. I won't go into the economics of that case here, except to say that it is widely accepted among economists that Social Security, whatever its virtues, discourages private saving and thus ultimately acts as a drag on economic growth. But any realistic proposal for Social Security reform must involve allocating additional money to the system to deal with the $10 trillion implicit debt.

Any reform of Social Security will require additional money *over and above the system's projected surplus*, because any reform would involve paying off some of that implicit debt. That is, Social Security reform would require using part of the non–Social Security surplus to help out the Social Security system. Here, by the way, is one place where the rhetoric of the administration is simply Orwellian. Again and again we hear that by allowing young workers to put some of their payroll taxes into private investment accounts we can "save Social Security." In fact, such accounts would *undermine* Social Security, because the benefits owed to older Americans must be paid out of those same taxes. If you want to partially privatize the Social Security system you need more tax revenue, not less.

The bottom line is that *at a minimum* a responsible policy now would be to consider the Social Security, Medicare, and pension fund surpluses off-limits, not available for tax cuts or new spending. And a truly responsible government, one that is honest about plans for Social Security reform, would set aside hundreds of billions of dollars over and above those surpluses to pay for its reform plans.

An Asset Test?

Right now money is accumulating in the Social Security and Medicare trust funds. But so far that money consists not of private-sector investments like stocks and corporate bonds but of the federal government's own debt, which the trust funds are buying from the public.

One sometimes hears people say that this means that the surpluses are phony—that because one part of the government is simply buying the debt of another part, money is simply being shuffled around. But if you think about it, that's not right. Debt owned by the trust funds is debt not owed to the public; and the less debt the federal government owes to the public, the lower the burden of interest payments on the budget. So paying down the debt today will make it easier for the government to pay benefits to the baby boomers a decade from now—it will not have to raise taxes or cut benefits as much as it otherwise would.

But if you accept, as you should, the proposition that the overall federal surplus over the next decade should be at least as large as the combined Social Security, Medicare, and pension fund surpluses over that period, you are led to the conclusion that those trust funds cannot continue to restrict themselves to buying only federal debt, because the federal debt is going to be eliminated. At this point there is only about $3.1 trillion in federal debt still in the hands of the public, while the projected combined surplus of the trust funds over the next decade is $3.3 trillion—more than the total quantity of debt. Furthermore, a fair amount, more than $1 trillion, of that outstanding debt will be hard to repay; it is subject to prepayment penalties, or it is held by institutions like foreign central banks that are unwilling to part with their claims on the U.S. government. So realistically the trust funds can only invest about $2 trillion more in federal debt.

Tax cut advocates have seized upon this limit to debt repayment as a reason to run a smaller surplus and give the money back in tax cuts instead. But that's a strange way to look at it. The fact that we may run out of federal debt does not change the arguments for building up reserves in the trust funds, and therefore does not change the argument for running a large surplus. What it does mean is that the trust funds should look into ways of investing their surpluses in assets other than federal debt.

Here's an analogy: consider that vigorous middle-aged couple, who have realized that they must save for their retirement. One thing they could do is pay off the mortgage on their house. But suppose it turns out that there are substantial prepayment penalties on the mortgage. Does that mean that they should give up on the idea of saving for their retirement? Shouldn't they simply adopt some other method of saving, such as buying stocks and bonds?

The answer is obvious: the couple should continue to save, buying assets instead of paying off the mortgage. And, correspondingly, the Social Security and Medicare systems should continue to build up their reserves, investing some of those reserves not in federal debt but in private assets.

Nonetheless, advocates of tax cuts have argued strongly against what seems to be the natural answer to the needs of the trust funds. Among them, alas, is Federal Reserve Chairman Alan Greenspan. In extremely influential testimony in February 2001 he argued that it would be dangerous to allow government agencies to buy private assets, because that would give politicians too much influence over the financial markets.

Experts on such matters were puzzled by that analysis, since there are well-known ways to insulate such investment decisions from politics. The simplest is to have the government agency invest automatically in a broad "index fund" that contains all major stocks and bonds, and to forbid the agency from taking an active role either in moving markets or in influencing corporate decisions. Such procedures are actually used all the time by state and local governments, whose pension plans currently own about $2 trillion in stocks and bonds.

In fact, when confronted by this argument, Mr. Greenspan seemed to retreat to a new line of defense; in later testimony he argued that even indexed investment by the government would distort the economy, because it would favor listed corporations over small, privately held businesses. And one must admit that he has a point. But it's a small point; given the choice between slightly skewing the allocation of capital between large and small business, and failing to make adequate preparation for the known burdens of an aging population, why would you choose to make the small bias in government investment your main concern?

All of which brings us to the bottom line: over the next decade the federal government ought to run a surplus of at least the $3.3 trillion projected by the trust funds, and a prudent policy would be to run a surplus considerably larger than that. Meanwhile, a realistic projection of the cumulative surplus over the next ten years on current policies, including Social Security and Medicare, is well under $5 trillion. So the amount really available for tax cuts, new spending plans, and so on is definitely less than $2 trillion. Auerbach and Gale put the number at between $1 trillion and $1.7 trillion; I'd put it lower. And given the inevitable uncertainty that surrounds such projections, a responsible government wouldn't lock in tax cuts even that big.

We need to keep that in mind when we turn to the tax cut plans that are actually on the table.

PART III

MAKING THE CUT

7

THE BUSH PLAN

THE BASICS

G IVE GEORGE W. BUSH points for consistency: his tax plan has remained almost unchanged since it was first conceived as a Forbes defense shield. In this chapter I will review some of the basics of the plan, and I will also turn to the key question of its affordability.

Three Tax Cuts

To get a rough picture of how the Bush tax plan works, it helps to realize that it really consists of three components that need not have any connection with one another. This is a point that the administration sometimes tries to conceal, insisting that the whole plan must be considered as a unified package; at other times the administration plays mix-and-match itself, presenting numbers that apply to only part of its plan. But more on that later.

Meanwhile, here are the three parts of the plan:

An Income Tax Reduction. When you fill out your 1040 form, you begin by calculating a series of exemptions, deductions, and credits; income after those exemptions and deductions is then taxed on a sliding scale that applies successively higher tax rates on higher levels of income. Most people either pay no income taxes or are in the 15 percent bracket. The highest tax bracket, which kicks in at an income in excess of $300,000 for a couple with two children, is 39.6 percent.

The Bush plan would reduce the tax rate within most of those brackets, and would also create a new bottom bracket for part of the range now taxed at a 15 percent rate. Table 3 summarizes the changes.

Table 3

CHANGES IN INCOME TAX RATES UNDER THE BUSH PROPOSAL (IN PERCENT)

Current bracket	Bush plan, 2006
na	→ 10*
15	→ 15
28	→ 25
31	→ 25
36	→ 33
39.6	→ 33

*new bottom bracket ("carve-out")

For families that do not pay income taxes, none of this would make any difference. For families near the middle of the income distribution, who currently pay a 15 percent rate on their taxable income, the effect of the Bush tax cut would be to reduce the tax rate on part of that income from 15 to 10 percent. This "carve-out" would apply to the first $6,000 of income for individuals, $12,000 for couples—so for median-income taxpayers the income tax cut would amount to either $300 or $600.

Meanwhile, the rate in the top tax bracket would be reduced from 39.6 to 33 percent. This means that very high-income families, most of whose income would fall into that top bracket, would get a tax break approaching 7 percent of their taxable income.

Overall, about half of the budget cost of the Bush tax plan, once it is fully phased in, would come from reductions in income tax rates.

A complicating feature of the Bush plan is that it would also try to reduce the "marriage penalty." This takes a bit of explaining. The income tax is "progressive"—that is, the tax rate is higher on taxpayers with higher incomes. But any progressive tax creates a dilemma: how do we calculate the tax bracket of married couples? Consider a couple with a combined income of $100,000: do we consider them to be in the $100,000 bracket, or do we put them in the $50,000 bracket, because income per adult is $50,000?

There is no perfect answer to this dilemma. In the 1960s, when the tax rate was based on income per adult, this led to complaints from relatively well-off widows: when their husbands died, their taxes suddenly went up. So Congress moved to a tax code that puts that $100,000 couple in a tax bracket that, though still lower than that of an unmarried individual making $100,000, was no longer as low as that of an individual making $50,000. For couples where only one member works, or where one member has a much higher income than the other, there is still a "marriage bonus"—the combined taxes the couple pays are less than they would pay if they weren't married. But if the incomes of the two partners are relatively equal, there is a "marriage penalty": if two individuals, each making $50,000, get married their taxes go up.

It turns out that roughly equal numbers of couples receive marriage bonuses and marriage penalties; but the penalty gets all the attention. So Bush has proposed a complicated set of changes that do not fully return the law to taxing on the basis of income per adult, but they do move it back in that direction. This adds somewhat to the budget cost of the plan. No doubt in some future decade this feature, too, will cause complaints, and around we will go.

The expanded child credit. The federal tax code already gives families a "tax credit"—that is, a sum that you can subtract not from your taxable income but from your taxes due—of $500 for every child under age 17. The Bush plan would double this credit, to $1000 per child.

This credit is not "refundable"—that is, if you don't pay

income taxes, you can't collect your $500. (There are some complicated exceptions involving child care expenses.) Since about one-third of children live in families that pay no income tax, this is a major exclusion.

For families near the middle of the income distribution, however, the expanded child credit could be a significant tax break—as long as they have enough children of the right age. The administration likes to talk about a "typical" family that gets a $1600 tax break. This is a family of four with two children still under 17; it gets $600 from the "carve-out," $1000 from the expanded child credit.

While the child credit is most of the benefit for this allegedly typical family, however, it accounts for only about 12 percent of the cost of the plan.

Eliminating the estate tax. Finally, the Bush plan calls for the eventual elimination of the estate tax and the closely related gift tax. We've already seen that the estate tax is mainly a tax on the seriously rich. The only point to add is that it would be a significant part of the Bush plan when that plan is fully phased in: nearly a quarter of the total. Recent Congressional estimates also suggest that eliminating the estate tax would have a large indirect cost to the Treasury, because it would offer wealthy individuals a number of new strategies for tax evasion. Administration officials say that they will find a way to close these loopholes, but at the time of writing they have not said how.

Tomorrow Is Another Day:
Back-Loading and the Cost of the Plan

In the last section I repeatedly used an annoying phrase: "when the plan is fully phased in." One of the important features of the Bush plan is the fact that the tax breaks come into effect with extreme gradualness.

In the plan, for example, that "carve-out" for the first $12,000 of a couple's income doesn't come next year. It comes at a percentage point per year, not arriving at the 10 percent level until 2006. The expanded child credit also arrives gradually; and the elimination of the estate tax is delayed even further, so that the entire plan would not be in place until 2008. The plan is heavily "back-loaded," with the big bucks arriving late in the game.

If tax cuts are a good idea, why phase them in so slowly? The obvious answer, of course, is that this keeps down the headline number, the ten-year cost of the plan. During the campaign the plan was billed as costing $1.3 trillion; now it's $1.6 trillion, but the administration insists that it will not go higher.

Actually, it already has gone higher, for a number of reasons. Here are a few of them:

- The House of Representatives modified the plan slightly, in ways that add to its cost.
- Since the plan was introduced, projections of economic

growth for the next decade have been raised. These upward revisions have increased the surplus projections made by the Congressional Budget Office. But higher income also means that tax cuts apply to a larger base, which means a bigger dollar figure.

• As Congressional staff members have gone over the specifics of the Bush proposal, they have consistently tended to find that the real cost of each tax break is higher than the administration claimed in its budget. Just as this book was being written, a blockbuster was dropped: Congressional staffers estimated that the tax loopholes created by elimination of the estate and gift taxes would add hundreds of billions to the cost of the Bush plan.

But back to the issue of back-loading. A key issue for the Bush program, though one that the media have never done a good job of reporting, is that a dollar of tax cuts is, in general, considerably more than a dollar deducted from those ten-year surplus projections. The reason is that if a dollar of surplus is used not to pay off debt but to offer a tax break, the government's interest payments in future years will be higher than they would have been otherwise. In fact, the budget effect grows through compound interest: a dollar of debt not paid off this year means a dollar plus interest of additional debt next year, and then interest on the dollar plus interest added for the next year, and so on. When you do the arithmetic, you find that a dollar refunded to taxpayers this year subtracts about $1.80 from the ten-year surplus.

This issue of interest costs is one that, as I've suggested, the administration has done a remarkably good job of obscuring so far as the media and the general public are concerned; they keep managing to talk about this as a $1.6 trillion tax cut. When submitting budget plans to Congress, however, the administration cannot simply pretend that the interest costs aren't there. These plans do show that when you include the impact of tax cuts on interest payments, that $1.6 trillion cut actually consumes about $2 trillion of the projected surplus.

But that number would be much larger if the tax cut weren't back-loaded. If the tax cut were put fully into effect in the first year, not only would the headline number be larger, but the extra financing cost would come early in the decade, meaning large indirect interest costs. So a back-loaded tax cut, in which much of the action doesn't happen until the second half of the decade, looks a lot cheaper.

Even so, estimates of the tax cut's budgetary cost keep rising; the number at the time of writing seemed to be at least $2.2 trillion, and the way things are going we can be sure that further examination will turn up a few hundred billion more of hidden costs.

And then there is the matter of the alternative minimum tax.

Running on AMT: The $300 Billion Sure Thing

Ever since Bush first proposed his tax cut during the campaign, tax analysts have warned that there was a lurking problem—a land mine in the road—involving the alternative minimum tax. The alternative minimum tax is an obscure corner of the tax code that won't stay obscure for much longer, because it will soon apply to many more people. And fixing the tax law to prevent that would subtract something like $130 billion from projected revenues over the next decade.

But if the Bush tax cut is enacted, the problem of the AMT would move to yet another level. Many taxpayers, mainly well-off but not rich people, would find that they aren't actually going to get the tax cuts they thought they had been promised, because they would find themselves paying the AMT instead.

How many people are we talking about? In March 2001 the bipartisan Joint Committee on Taxation estimated that under the Bush plan *1 in 3* taxpayers would find themselves subject to the alternative minimum tax.

Don't worry; this isn't going to happen. It is a sure thing that long before the AMT became an issue for so many people the tax plan would be subject to a "fix" that would prevent that result. This is a fix over and above the fix we discussed in Chapter 6, which was designed to prevent the AMT from becoming a mass issue under *current* tax law.

So how much extra would it cost to fix the AMT under the Bush proposal? The committee answered that too, with the spurious precision typical of this subject: $292 billion. Let's say $300 billion—the $300 billion sure thing.

The Bush Gap

We are now finally closing in on our first big question about the Bush tax plan: does it really make fiscal sense? Can we really afford this?

It won't surprise you to hear that the answer is no. But let's walk through this a bit.

At the time of writing, a *conservative* estimate—that's financial conservatism, not political—of the ten-year budget cost of the Bush tax cut is $2.5 trillion. It's a good bet that as the details of the plan continue to be examined, that cost will go higher; indeed, the report by the Joint Committee on Taxation that the repeal of the estate tax will provide opportunities for evasion of other taxes suggests that the cost may already be at $2.7 trillion and counting. But let's be kind and gentle to Mr. Bush and suppose for the sake of argument that it is really only $2.5 trillion.

Meanwhile, a *generous* estimate of the amount of money that the federal government can responsibly use for tax cuts and new spending programs combined is $2 trillion. As we've seen, there are very good reasons to think that this figure is considerably too high, that a realistic number could be $1 trillion or less. But again, let's take the most favorable case.

What we are left with, then, is that even on highly favorable assumptions we have a $2.5 trillion tax cut, and only $2 trillion of available funds; so there is a shortfall of $500 billion. And that is without considering new programs.

But that is not the way the White House describes the situation. Indeed, in his speech to Congress describing his budget plans, Bush claimed that he could afford the tax cut so easily that he was setting aside a "trillion-dollar contingency fund" over and above his tax cutting and spending plans.

It turns out that Bush was exercising poetic license; the real size of that contingency fund is $842 billion. Even so, there is a large difference between our estimate that even under highly favorable assumptions, the Bush tax cut creates a $500 billion shortfall and Bush's claim that he has $800 billion to spare. What are the sources of this $1.3 trillion "Bush gap"?

Actually, it's pretty simple. There are only three main pieces:

- Bush underestimates the budget cost of his tax cut by at least $500 billion. The administration's figures continue to cost the proposal at about $2 trillion including interest, ignoring the Congressional revisions that put the number $200 billion higher, and the certainty that a fix for the alternative minimum tax will add another $300 billion.

- The surplus number is based on unreasonable spending projections. We saw in Chapter 5 that the CBO projection assumes no growth in discretionary spending, which is a 10 percent decline per capita—and this would require a severe and unrealistic shrinkage of the government's role. Keeping spending per capita unchanged—still a quite conservative policy—would reduce the funds available by another $400 billion.

- Bush counts $400 billion of Medicare surpluses in his "contingency fund." In effect, he plans to raid Medicare to pay for tax cuts.

This last point needs some explanation because it is a politically explosive statement and also because the administration has already prepared a specious but cleverly confusing defense involving the definition of "Medicare."

It turns out that Medicare officially consists of two programs. Part A, hospital insurance, is the program paid for with the payroll tax; it is also the part of the program that is running a surplus, in preparation for the retirement of the baby boomers. Part B, supplementary medical insurance, is paid for by a mix of fees from Medicare recipients and general (not payroll) tax revenues. Part A has a trust fund; Part B does not. So Part B, although it is run by the Medicare system, is really part of the non-Medicare budget.

The Bush program calls for diverting some of the payroll taxes that have until now been reserved for Part A, and have been used to accumulate a trust fund, to pay for current Part B expenses. By reducing the amount of general revenue needed to support Part B, this would free up money for tax cuts. This is in effect a raid on the Medicare trust fund: every dollar of money diverted from Part A to Part B is one dollar less saved to deal with the future medical expenses of the baby boomers. Technically the administration can say, and has said, that Medicare funds are being used only for Medicare. But the important point is that funds that were supposed to be set aside to provide for future Medicare recipients are instead being used to make room in the budget for tax cuts. If you find it hard to believe that the leaders of a great nation would resort to such tricks—well, you just don't understand how important it is to get that tax cut.

Among the uses to which the diverted Medicare trust fund money will be put is a new prescription drug program for seniors—which brings us to a different if fuzzier Bush gap, this time involving the cost of new programs.

Sects and Drugs and Rockets' Role

Candidate Bush didn't run only on the promise of tax cuts. He ran also on a platform that promised new social programs as part of his "compassionate conservatism," a prescription drug program for seniors, and a strengthened military.

We can probably forget about the social programs; all indications are that as soon as he entered the White House Bush dropped the first three letters from his "compassionate" conservatism. The one distinctive initiative, the idea of delivering money through "faith-based" programs, has been losing momentum; it has apparently suddenly dawned on Washington that the Constitution does not allow us to write a law that restricts a program to nice Judeo-Christian organizations, and that well-organized sects like the Nation of Islam, Hare Krishna, and Scientology would if anything be better placed than Baptists or Episcopalians to get funds.

The Bush administration has also delivered a rude shock to

the military, which was expecting lots of money and has been told to expect no real increase. It's unclear whether this is really the administration's long-run policy—whether all that campaign rhetoric about the alarming weakness of the military was insincere—or whether it is simply a tactical move to make the surplus look bigger until the tax cut has been enacted. It's also unclear how the administration proposes to pay for the rockets: the promised missile defense system, whose cost has never been in its budget estimates.

One thing we do know, however, is that the administration's promise on drugs is going to be much more expensive than the $150 billion its budget has allotted. Congressional staff estimates put the cost at at least twice that, and probably much more.

Why is the administration's estimate considered so unrealistic? Partly because almost nobody who has studied the problem of providing drug coverage believes in the fundamental logic of the Bush plan, which assumes that drug coverage can be achieved on the cheap by subsidizing insurance companies who provide coverage rather than insuring individuals directly. There's even a case study. When the state of Nevada tried to implement a plan along similar lines, it found no licensed insurance companies willing to participate in what was a clear money-losing proposition.

There's also a larger issue. Although upward revisions in the projected budget surplus have been making headlines recently, another kind of less-noticed upward revision has been taking place: projections of future medical costs in general, and of the burden of those medical costs on the federal budget, have been rising.

Rising medical costs have been a consistent feature of the U.S. economy, and of the federal budget, for decades. The main reason isn't inflation; it's the advance of medical science. There are simply more useful things that doctors can do. For a while during the 1990s this upward trend flattened out, as the rise of HMOs squeezed medical fees. But the big squeeze is over— HMOs can't get any more tight-fisted than they already are— and medical costs have resumed their upward march. Many budget analysts believe that as a result the long-run federal budget picture, looking beyond that ten-year horizon, has actually gotten worse over the past year.

Trying to add up all of these factors is an exercise in utterly fuzzy math. My crude guesstimate is that a reasonable forecast of the ten-year surplus if the Bush plan is put into effect is no more than $2 trillion—that is, well over $1 trillion less than the minimum responsible surplus. The administration continues to claim that the tax cut can easily be afforded but, as the costs of its promises mount, that claim looks not just silly but disingenuous.

8

FOR RICHER, FOR POORER

WHO BENEFITS FROM THE TAX CUT?

FEW ISSUES SURROUNDING the Bush tax cut have raised tempers higher than the question of who gets most of the benefits. Is it, as critics have charged, mainly a tax cut for the rich? Or are the calculations behind these charges "fuzzy math," and are the critics engaged in disreputable "class warfare"?

It's a strange dispute, because the distribution of the benefits is not hard to calculate. The data are readily available; all you have to do is plug in the tax plan and ask whose taxes would fall by how much. But politics does strange things to analysis: while some participants in the debate have done the straightforward calculations, others—including the Treasury department—have come up with complicated and peculiar ways to approach the subject, and have produced results that seem to conflict with the straightforward assessment.

All in the Families

Let's give credit where credit is due: those "tax families" were a brilliant marketing idea. Both during the campaign to win the White House and in the subsequent campaign to pass the tax cut, the Bush team rolled out photogenic, all-American families who would gain from the tax cut to show that their plan wasn't about the rich, but was about all of us. And even when not doing photo-ops, the Bush people insistently frame their sales pitch in terms of a "typical" family. This family has two adults and two children, earns $40,000 per year, and will receive a $1600 tax cut.

What's brilliant about all of this is the way it takes advantage of basic human instincts. We are all hard-wired to react more strongly to personal anecdotes than to dry statistics; we are also inclined to view our society through Norman Rockwell lenses. A picture of a real family is much more persuasive to most people than a table of numbers; and most of us, when asked to imagine a typical American family, imagine the way we would *like* the typical family to be, not the way it really is.

So what's wrong with this picture? As far as it goes, it's entirely accurate: a family of 4, with both children under age 17, earning $40,000 per year, will indeed get a $1600 tax cut: $600 from the "carve-out" in the tax schedule, $1000 from expanded child credits. But look at different families—and there are many different kinds of families—and you get very different pictures.

Suppose, for example, that we consider a couple with the

same income, but without those two children; maybe they haven't had children yet, maybe the children are grown. Then they don't get the child credits, so the tax break drops to $600. A single adult with the same income—someone not yet married or divorced, a widow or widower—gets only $300.

Or suppose that the family's income is smaller—say, $30,000. Then it will pay only about $750 in income taxes under current law, although it pays more than $5000 in payroll taxes. Under the Bush plan you can't, except in some special cases, actually get back more than you pay in income tax; so for a family a bit poorer than the idealized "tax family" the tax cut drops to $750, even if the family has the ideal number of adults and children.

And so on. That "typical" family turns out not to be typical at all. In fact, barely one-tenth of the nation's families would actually get as much as that "typical" tax cut.

Maybe the moral of this is that when it comes to the middle class, the whole idea of the tax cut for a typical family is a nonstarter. Because of the way the Bush tax cut is set up, the size of the tax cut a middle-income family gets depends on the fine print: whether you are a married couple, whether you have enough children the right age. The families displayed by the administration are carefully chosen to make the tax cut look good.

However, while the picture is complicated for middle-income families, it is simple for both the rich and the poor. The poor get nothing, and even the lower middle class gets only a token cut. The reason is that low-income families pay little or no income tax, though they may pay plenty of payroll taxes, and so they get little break on rates and aren't eligible for the full child credit.

Meanwhile, the rich are also guaranteed a large cut, regardless of the composition of their families, because of that reduction in the rate on the top bracket from 39.6 to 33 percent. The only important variation among rich families is between the new rich, who will not be receiving large inheritances, and the old rich, who will; the latter will get a big additional tax cut because of the elimination of the estate tax.

So that's the picture: nothing for the poor; significant tax cuts for middle-income families with children the right age, but minor cuts otherwise; big tax cuts for the rich, more or less regardless of family details. Why, then, do some estimates seem to tell a different story?

A Tale of Three Tables

In the good old days—before George Bush was inaugurated in January 2001—the U.S. Treasury department used to provide detailed information about the effects of proposed tax law changes on different income groups. If you go further back, before the Republican takeover of Congress in 1994, the House Ways and Means Committee used to do the same thing. But both now refuse to provide those calculations to the public.

What we're left with, then, are think tanks. The two key players in this debate are the Center on Budget and Policy Priorities and Citizens for Tax Justice (check them out on the Web at www.cbpp.org and www.ctj.org—both sites offer lots of useful information).

Given the nastiness of the political debate, one must answer the question, aren't these "liberal" think tanks? And the answer is yes, sort of; certainly both tend to be critical of tax cut plans and both care about the distribution of income, which in modern American politics makes them "liberal." I would present alternative numbers from conservative think tanks, but conservative think tanks refuse even to address the questions CBPP and CTJ answer.

The real question, though, is whether the numbers these groups produce have been cooked—that is, whether the data have been falsified. And the answer is a definite no; the way that CTJ and CBPP make their calculations is identical to the way that Treasury used to do similar exercises, and is based on more or less the same data. In fact, it's almost certain that Treasury *has* done the same calculations, and gotten more or less the same results—it just won't release those results. Some people have suggested that Treasury Secretary Paul O'Neill should be sued under the Freedom of Information Act and forced to reveal what his staff knows.

Anyway, on to the numbers. The first thing we need to do is get an idea of what we're talking about when we look at different income groups. Table 4 shows the breakdown used by both CTJ and CBPP. They look at income by "quintiles"—that is, the population broken into five equal-sized groups: the poorest 20 percent, the next poorest 20 percent, and so on. They also subdivide the top quintile of families into the top 1 percent, the next 4 percent, and the next 15 percent. The table shows the income ranges for each group and the average income within each group. (These numbers are from Citizens for Tax

Justice, but they are surely accurate: in 1999 the Congressional Budget Office provided income estimates for the same groupings that matched very closely CTJ's numbers for that year.)

The key lesson of this table is to be clear what we mean when talking about whether tax cuts favor the "rich." Conservatives who are willing to talk about income distribution at all typically refuse to talk about any subdivisions of the top 20 percent. That is, they refuse to talk about how income is divided *among* the richest 20 percent of the population. The O'Neill Treasury department was slightly more forthcoming, offering data on the effect of the tax cut on people with incomes of more than $200,000. But that does not count as rich anymore; America's rich, in this new millennium, are really, really rich. The top 1 percent category that has become the focus of much discussion consists of families with a minimum income of $373,000 and an *average* income of more than $1.1 million.

According to the think tanks, these seriously rich families are

Table 4

INCOME GROUPS USED FOR EVALUATING THE BUSH TAX PLAN		
Income group	Income range	Average income
Lowest 20 percent	less than $15,000	$9,300
Second 20 percent	$15,000–$27,000	$20,600
Middle 20 percent	$27,000–$44,000	$34,400
Fourth 20 percent	$44,000–$72,000	$56,400
Next 15 percent	$72,000–$147,000	$97,400
Next 4 percent	$147,000–$373,000	$210,000
Top 1 percent	more than $373,000	$1,117,000

Source: Citizens for Tax Justice.

the big winners from the Bush tax plan. Tables 5 and 6 show estimates from CTJ and CBPP of what the tax cuts for different groups would be if the Bush plan were in effect right now.

Table 5 shows how CTJ likes to think about the issue: it shows their estimates of the average dollar tax cut for families in each group, and it also shows the share of the total tax cut that would go to each group. This is a tax cut dramatically tilted toward the seriously rich: the top 1 percent of taxpayers gets 45 percent of the total tax break. CBPP has made a slightly lower but similar estimate: 39 percent.

Table 6 shows how CBPP likes to think about the issue: it shows estimates of how much the after-tax income of each group would rise as a result of the Bush plan. This table, too, suggests a tax cut that disproportionately benefits the rich. Poor families would see almost no increase in their income; middle-income families would on average see their after-tax incomes rise about 2 percent; the top 1 percent of families would see a gain of more than 6 percent.

Table 5

THE DISTRIBUTION OF THE BUSH TAX CUTS: ONE VIEW

Income group	Average dollar cut	Percentage of total tax cut
Bottom 20%	$47	0.8
Second 20%	$212	3.5
Third 20%	$509	8.4
Fourth 20%	$951	15.7
Next 15%	$1,523	18.9
Next 4%	$2,356	7.8
Top 1%	$54,480	45.0

Source: Citizens for Tax Justice.

Table 6

THE DISTRIBUTION OF THE BUSH TAX CUTS: ANOTHER VIEW	
Income group	Percent increase in after-tax income
Lowest 20%	0.6
Next 20%	1.2
Middle 20%	1.9
Next 20%	2.3
Next 15%	2.4
Next 4%	2.4
Top 1%	6.2

Source: Center on Budget and Policy Priorities.

This is pretty explosive stuff; so to counter it the administration put out its own estimates, which seem very different. But the operative word is "seem."

Table 7 shows the estimates circulated by the Treasury department. They break income down differently, showing income ranges rather than a percentage distribution of fami-

Table 7

THE DISTRIBUTION OF THE BUSH TAX CUTS: THE TREASURY TABLE		
Cash income ($ thousands)	Share of income tax cut	Percent change in income taxes
0–30	9.3	-136.2
30–40	6.5	-38.3
40–50	7.8	-28.0
50–75	17.2	-20.8
75–100	13.6	-16.3
100–200	19.8	-10.7
>200	25.4	-8.7

lies. For each income range the Treasury table shows the percentage reduction in income taxes and the share of the total income tax reduction that goes to each group. These look very different: it seems as if a much smaller share of the tax break goes to the rich than CTJ calculated, and it also seems as if taxes fall more for the poor and the middle class than they do for the rich. In other words, it seems as if Treasury is saying that the numbers provided by CTJ and CBPP, which we saw in those last two tables, are all wrong.

But it's an illusion. *The Treasury estimates are almost the same as those of the "liberal" think tanks.* The difference between Table 7 and the previous two tables is a matter of packaging. To be blunt, the Treasury table is a classic demonstration of "how to lie with statistics," presenting true numbers in such a way as to suggest an untrue conclusion.

How can the numbers in Table 7, which look so different from those in Tables 5 and 6, really be the same? The sleight of hand involves two main tricks.

First, the Treasury estimates are not for the entire Bush plan; they are only for the *income* tax reductions, including the child credit. That means that they leave out the effect of eliminating the estate tax. Now remember that the estate tax elimination isn't a small feature of the Bush tax cut—it's about a quarter of the total cost. And because the estate tax falls mainly on a tiny handful of multi-million-dollar estates, the benefits are almost entirely concentrated within the Treasury's top category. Add in the estate tax to the Treasury calculations, and about 45 percent of the benefits of the tax cut would go to the "over $200,000" category. In other words, the table would look a lot like Table 5.

Second, the Treasury doesn't calculate the income tax reduction as a percentage of *income*; it calculates it as a percentage of *income taxes paid*. Remember from Chapter 3 that low- and middle-income families pay only a small share of their income in income taxes, though they pay a large share in payroll taxes; for high-income families the reverse is true. What this means is that dividing the tax cuts by income taxes rather than income makes big tax cuts for the rich seem small and tax cuts for poorer families look big.

This seems to be a tricky point to explain, but maybe it will be clear if we go straight to the numbers. The Treasury table says that families with incomes in the $30,000–$40,000 range will get about a 40 percent cut in income taxes; but families in that range typically pay *income* (as opposed to *total*) taxes that are only about 5 percent of their after-tax income, so this is roughly only a 2 percent increase in after-tax income. Meanwhile, income taxes on high-income families are usually more than 30 percent of after-tax income, so the 9 percent reduction shown in the Treasury table would mean an increase in after-tax income of almost 3 percent. Add in the effects of eliminating the estate tax, and you end up with numbers more or less the same as Table 6.

Because the Treasury's income categories don't correspond to the categories used by the think tanks—which happen to be the same categories the Treasury department itself always used until now—you can't demonstrate directly that the underlying numbers in Table 7 are more or less the same as those in Tables 5 and 6. But you can come pretty close. Table 8 compares the Treasury numbers for two groups with roughly comparable groups used by CTJ. Notice that the top Treasury group more nearly corresponds to the top 5 percent of the CTJ table than the top 1 percent—that is, the Treasury category is actually quite broad because it doesn't separate the really rich from the merely affluent. And while the Treasury doesn't give actual dollar tax cut numbers, it does gives you enough information to work out what the hidden dollar numbers are. Sure enough, the Treasury numbers don't look very different from the CTJ estimates.

Now you might still think that the numbers in Table 8 don't look quite as startling as those in Table 5—a tax cut of $10,000 per rich family isn't quite as shocking as a tax cut of more than $50,000. But there isn't any real conflict between the numbers. The category of families with incomes of $200,000 and over mixes the merely well-off with the truly rich, diluting the huge tax breaks that million-dollar-plus families receive; also, the Treasury estimate ignores the effect of eliminating the estate tax, which doubles the total.

This distinction between the rich and the merely well-off is an important one. Film buffs may recall a scene in the

Table 8

COMPARING THE TREASURY WITH CITIZENS FOR TAX JUSTICE	
Treasury estimate of dollar income tax reduction:	
Families with incomes of $30–40,000	$616
Families with incomes of more than $200,000	$9,903
Citizens for Tax Justice estimates of dollar income tax reduction:	
Families in middle 20% (incomes between $27,000 and $44,000)	$500
Families in top 5% (incomes greater than $147,000)	$7,050

Source: U.S. Treasury Department, Citizens for Tax Justice, author's calculations.

movie *Wall Street* in which Michael Douglas (playing financial predator Gordon Gekko) says, "I'm not talking about some $400,000 a year working Wall Street stiff flying first class and being comfortable." It turns out that the Bush tax plan is not that great a deal for those "working stiffs"; its really big benefits go only to those Gekko described as "players." The Citizens for Tax Justice estimates suggest that of the total tax cuts that go to the top 5 percent of taxpayers, the great bulk—more than 85 percent—would go to the top 1 percent.

One reason why the tax cut favors the really rich more than the merely comfortable is the estate tax repeal; even $400,000 a year working stiffs don't usually inherit $10 million estates. The other is—you may have guessed this—the alternative minimum tax. Again, according to Citizens for Tax Justice, families in the top 5 percent but not in the top 1 percent would find that *two-thirds* of their apparent gain from the Bush income tax cuts is snatched away by the alternative minimum tax.

In the end, then, there really isn't any disagreement over the facts. What we know about the Bush tax plan is the following:

1. *A large fraction of the tax cut goes to a small number of families.* Any way you look at it, about 40 percent, plus or minus a few percent, of the total tax cut would go to the top 1 percent of the income distribution. The Treasury numbers, if you look at them carefully, actually confirm this conclusion.

2. *The after-tax income of the rich will rise much more, as a percentage of their current income, than that of the middle class or the poor.* The average family in the top 1 percent would find its purchasing power increased by around 6 percent, compared with

2 percent for middle-income families and much less than 1 percent for the poor. Again, the Treasury numbers, read carefully, confirm this conclusion.

3. *The income taxes of the rich will fall less, as a percentage of their income taxes, than those of the middle class or the poor.* The "liberal" think tanks never disputed this proposition. What they would say is that it misses the point.

Lies, Damn Lies, and Statistics

Since there is no real disagreement about the facts of the Bush tax cut, the difference between the think tanks and the Treasury comes down to a difference of interpretation. What do we mean when we say that a tax cut is tilted toward the rich?

One answer is that the tax cut would raise the standard of living of the rich more than it would raise the standard of living of the middle class or the poor. And that is clearly true, because the rich would see a much larger percentage increase in their after-tax income.

Another answer is that a large part of the budget cost of the tax cut would benefit a small number of wealthy people. And that is also clearly true, because around 40 percent of the tax cut would definitely go to the top 1 percent of families.

The Treasury, however, claims that the tax cut isn't tilted to the rich, because their income taxes would fall by a smaller percentage.

It helps to think about the raw numbers involved. All three studies agree that, on average, families with an income of $35,000 per year would get tax reductions of around $600 per year, and that, on average, families with an income of $1,000,000 per year would get income tax breaks of around $25,000; add in the estate tax repeal and that last number becomes $50,000. But the Treasury table leaves out the estate tax repeal and presents the income tax numbers in such a way that the $600 break seems "bigger."

Nobody confronted with the actual numbers would accept this interpretation, and the Treasury department knows that nobody would accept it. That's why their table suppresses all the information that would make it easy to see what is really going on. They ignore a crucial piece of the administration's tax proposal; they hide the raw dollar figures; they don't tell you how many families there are in each income class; and they choose a set of income categories that mingles the big beneficiaries of the tax cut with merely comfortable "working stiffs" whose tax cuts are largely snatched away by the alternative minimum tax.

Not only is the tax cut tilted toward the rich by any normal measure. The administration has also deliberately tried to confuse the public. This is not just an issue of policy; it's an issue of honesty.

9

ALTERNATIVES

THE OBJECTIONS TO the Bush tax plan are straightforward. It appears to be irresponsibly large in that it would prevent the federal government from setting aside sufficient reserves to deal with the retirement of the baby boomers. It is also, despite contrary claims by its supporters, very tilted toward the rich; even the administration's own estimates, once you peel away the misleading packaging, confirm the proposition that around 40 percent of the benefits will go to the richest 1 percent of taxpayers.

Meanwhile, the administration's favorite sales pitch over the past few months—that the tax cut must be passed to stimulate a slowing economy—is at odds with the structure of the plan, which is heavily back-loaded and delivers very little money to consumers in the near term.

But suppose that you accept that this plan is ill-conceived. What are the alternatives?

The Zero Option

There is, believe it or not, a good economic case to be made for no tax cut at all. Politically this seems to be outside the realm of the possible, but it's worth understanding why it might make economic sense.

It comes down, once again, to the nature of the modern federal government, to the fact that it has become a retirement state governing an aging population. Add to this the rising cost of medical care, and the long-run budget position of the U.S. government—looking beyond the ten-year horizon—starts to look quite bleak. Economists who do long-range versions of the CBO exercise, projecting the federal budget under the assumption of "current policy"—together with heroic guesses about future economic conditions—generally find that taxes will have to be raised, benefits cut, or both.

There's another way to look at it, which arrives at the same conclusion. The long-run U.S. budget problem is the result of the way we have run our social insurance programs for retirees, treating them as pay-as-you-go systems rather than accumulating assets the way we would have to if they were private plans. So there is a case for converting both Social Security and Medicare to fully funded systems—not necessarily privatizing them, though that would be one way to do it, but in one way or another making them adhere to the same financial standards that private retirement and health plans obey. To switch to full funding would, however, require providing enough money to pay off the unfunded liabilities of the systems: $10 trillion for Social Security, trillions more for Medicare. Allocating *all* of the projected surplus for the next decade to that purpose would be only a start on this project; so again you can argue that no tax cut at all is warranted.

This zero option has largely vanished from the debate; even those politicians who agree with this position intellectually regard it as indefensible politically. But it is a reason to regard smaller as better when it comes to tax cut proposals that might actually be adopted.

Smaller, Cheaper, Faster, Better?

In the early 1990s, after some big-budget fiascoes, the National Aeronautics and Space Administration embraced a new strategy of "smaller, cheaper, faster, better" missions. The results of that strategy have been mixed, but the slogan serves quite well to describe the main alternative to the Bush plan that has emerged this year.

As of early April 2001, when this book went to press, Democrats had agreed on their alternative, which certainly embodied the first three words in the NASA slogan. It contained only two pieces:

- a $300 rebate to each taxpayer this year
- a quick—not phased—implementation of the Bush "carve-out," reducing the tax rate on the first $6,000 of income for individuals, $12,000 for couples, from 15 to 10 percent.

For those taxpayers who are above the 15 percent bracket—

about one taxpayer in four—this would certainly be a *smaller* cut than the Bush proposal. That is also the reason why the Democratic cut, although it would not be back-loaded to keep the cost down, would still be much *cheaper* than the Bush plan—less than $500 billion. It would arrive *faster*—the rebate would put $60 billion in the hands of consumers this year— and the carve-out would not take 5 years to fully phase in.

But is this plan *better*? Bush and his aides have energetically denounced the Democratic plan, on two main economic grounds.

Their first objection is that a one-time rebate will not lead to much of an increase in consumer spending—that to boost spending now we must implement a permanent tax cut. There is actually a well-known economic rationale for that position: the so-called "permanent income hypothesis," due to none other than Milton Friedman. This says that rational consumers should base their spending not on this year's income but on what they expect their income to be over the long run, smoothing out temporary ups and downs. Permanent income reasoning suggests that consumers, realizing that the Democratic tax rebate is a one-time thing, would save it rather than spend it.

We might note as an aside that if this is the way the Bush people really view the economy, the attempt to sell their tax cut as a recession-fighting measure has very peculiar long-term policy implications. Are we supposed to fight every temporary economic downturn with a permanent tax cut? Doesn't that mean a tax rate that ratchets down every time there is a slowdown? Or are we supposed to raise rates again when the economy is booming—and in that case in what sense are the tax changes permanent? I'm getting dizzy.

But there is considerable evidence that the administration has the economics wrong. Friedman's permanent income hypothesis has been the subject of a huge body of statistical research, and the claim that current income has no effect on spending has been decisively rejected. People do base their spending in part on long-run expectations of income, but they also respond to short-run changes in their income to a much greater extent than Friedman's theory would suggest.

One reason why short-run income matters a lot is that many consumers are cash-constrained: they cannot borrow, or can do so only at high interest rates, so they cannot currently spend as much as their long-run income prospects warrant. Such consumers would therefore spend most or all of a rebate; and because poor and lower-middle-income families would get the same rebate as the affluent, much of the money would actually go to people in that position.

Aside from the general evidence that consumer spending does respond to short-run movements in income, there is some prior experience with rebates as a recession-fighting measure. A similar rebate was tried during the Ford administration. Did it work? It depends on whom you ask. Treasury Secretary Paul O'Neill told the National Association of Business Economists that the Ford rebate was a failure: "Some have suggested we send a rebate to the taxpayers now and stop there. That's not good enough. I was here when we tried that in 1975 and it didn't work. If we want to change consumption patterns, we need to make a permanent change in people's tax burdens." But many economists disagree; several studies have found evidence that the Ford rebate did indeed stimulate consumer spending.

There's still the argument that a tax stimulus to consumption is unnecessary, that the Fed can and will do the job with interest rate cuts. I personally believe that that's true, that the economy will recover with or without an immediate fiscal stimulus. But that argument applies with equal force to the attempt to sell the Bush plan as a recession-fighting measure. Meanwhile, the rebate would be cheap, compared with the numbers we have been talking about, so why not?

The second objection raised by the administration to the Democratic plan—although it has not been expressed very loudly—is that the plan would by and large not reduce *marginal* tax rates. Except for those families whose taxable income is insufficient to allow them to claim the full carve-out, this plan would not reduce the taxes paid on an *additional* dollar of income. So there would be no improvement in supply-side incentives.

The administration would be in a better position to make this objection if it had ever tried to sell its plan for what it really is. The best case you can make for the Bush plan is one that owns up to the plan's supply-side origins and admits that the plan offers by far its biggest benefits to people with high incomes; the reduction in the top marginal tax rate from 39.6 percent to 33 percent is significant, and the elimination of the estate tax would be a significant further incentive for those who hope to pass multi-million-dollar estates on to their children (though all that tax-free inherited wealth would substantially reduce the incentives for the children of the wealthy to emulate the initiative of their parents).

But that is never the way the plan has been sold. In fact, the most conspicuous thing about that "typical" family earning $40,000 and receiving a $1600 tax break, aside from the fact that it isn't typical, is that *it receives no supply-side incentives from the Bush tax plan*: the marginal tax rate facing that "typical" family stays at 15 percent.

In any case, even if the administration were willing to make a fully fledged supply-side case for its plan, there would be no good reason to take that case seriously. As pointed out in Chapter 2, the U.S. economy did not experience an acceleration of growth in its productive capacity after Reagan cut marginal tax rates in the 1980s; it *did* experience such an acceleration after Clinton *raised* that top marginal rate in the 1990s. Furthermore, what we are experiencing now is a demand-side slowdown; as far as we can tell, the great productivity boom that began in 1995 is still continuing.

Nonetheless, though the administration has not been willing to make a fully fledged supply-side case for its plan, the supply-siders are still out there; and some Republicans in Congress are pushing for a much bigger tax cut.

Is There a Case for an Even Bigger Tax Cut?

In late March 2001 three of the four top Republicans in the House, including Majority Leader Dick Armey and Majority Whip Tom DeLay, endorsed a proposal for a tax cut with a headline cost of $2.2 trillion over the next decade. Everything I've said about why the true budget impact of the Bush tax cut is larger than the headline number applies with equal force to this proposal, so you should think of it as a tax cut of, say, $3.3 trillion.

If one stays with the CBO projection, the only way to afford a tax cut this large would be either to cut deeply into the Social Security and Medicare trust funds or to slash discretionary spending per capita to levels not seen since the 1930s. So what is the rationale for such large cuts?

The economic answer comes in two parts. Advocates of really big tax cuts believe that over the next decade the U.S. economy can grow at rates comparable to its performance during the second half of the 1990s, delivering trillions of dollars in additional revenue. And that's certainly possible, though a decade of growth at that rate would be unprecedented in U.S. history. But why would you want to lock yourself into a budget that makes the risky assumption that the remarkable boom of the last five years will continue unabated for the next ten?

The second part of the economic answer is that true believers in supply-side economics believe that they can *make* the boom continue by cutting tax rates at the top. It's hard to see what in the evidence makes them believe that, but they do; call it faith-based economic policy.

Why Not Compromise?

I end this book with political speculation. Because of the physical lags involved in putting out a book, anything I write about the politics of the tax cut is at great risk of being overtaken by events. By the time you read this, it is possible that momentum for the Bush tax plan will have collapsed, or that a coordinated rush will have made passage of the plan in its entirety a done deal. It's also possible that Bush will have accepted a compromise that gives him only part of his plan, with the hope that he can get the rest through later.

Indeed, the Democratic alternative actually fits that description. Aside from the one-time rebate, it consists of one element from the Bush plan, the carve-out for middle-income taxpayers. So why can't Bush say okay, that's a start, and go on from there? Or why not drop some of the most objectionable elements from his plan—the estate tax repeal, the big cut in income tax rates for the top bracket—in order to make the plan both cheaper and more palatable to moderates?

It could happen, and as an amateur when it comes to political analysis, I can't say it won't happen. But I believe that Bush is unlikely to give in, for reasons that go back to the discussion of the politics of tax cuts in Chapter 1.

First, Bush himself is still trying to escape from his father's shadow; a compromise might cause the right to turn on him.

Second, timing is everything. Right now Bush is trying to rush his program through, making use both of fears of a weakening economy and of the political capital that a new president, even one who lost the popular vote, possesses. If Congress is allowed to vote separately on the parts of the package that moderates find acceptable, it will be much less inclined to rush the rest. And as the months go by, the economy will probably improve, and the hidden costs of the plan will become more obvious. If the debate drags on into next year, those ten-year projections will start to incorporate the leading edge of the wave of retiring baby boomers, and the game will probably be up.

Third, a tax cut we can easily afford is exactly what conservatives don't want. Most of the people I know who support the

Bush tax plan support it precisely because they think it will squeeze the budget, forcing cutbacks in social programs. (None of them are politicians, who would be smart enough not to say such things, at least not when I'm around.) A downsized version of the Bush tax plan would therefore not be acceptable.

Finally, there's the matter of the "deep" conservative agenda. To the extent that this governs the conservative strategy, it would make the administration completely unwilling to accept a compromise plan that reduces the current plan's tilt toward the rich.

Think of it this way: suppose that your long-term strategy is to ensure that middle-income voters see the government as a burden, not as a source of benefits. A tax cut that reduces taxes on middle-income families more than it reduces taxes on the rich doesn't work in favor of that strategy; it works against it, because tax revenue won't fall enough to force large cuts in benefits, while the median voter will actually find government less burdensome and therefore look on it more kindly. So to serve its long-term goal the tax cut *must* be tilted toward the rich; compromising on this would miss the point.

Let me conclude on a personal note. It is obvious from everything in this book that I am opposed to the Bush tax cut. A lot of this opposition is on economic grounds: I believe that the plan would compromise our long-term fiscal integrity. I am also one of the people who thinks that most of the money spent by the U.S. government does a lot of real good; it's a value judgment, but I don't accept the idea that our government is too big and should be made much smaller.

But there's a special reason to oppose the Bush plan, quite

aside from its actual merits or lack thereof. This is the utter dishonesty of the sales campaign. At every stage of this debate Bush and his people have tried to obscure what they were really proposing. They have radically understated the cost of their plan while overstating the money available to pay that cost. They have pretended that a plan that mainly cuts taxes for the extremely well off is basically a middle-class tax cut, and they have misrepresented the size of the tax cut that middle-income families will actually receive. And they have falsely sold the plan as an appropriate answer to a short-run economic slowdown, when it is almost perfectly designed *not* to deal with that sort of problem.

I can't think of any previous administration that has tried to sell its economic plans on such false pretenses. It would be a shame, and a dangerous precedent, if they get away with it.